Tales of a Traveling Soul

A Memoir by Julie Douat Brand

Acknowledgments

I would like to express my gratitude to the special people in my life who saw me through the writing of this book. I would like to thank my good friend Franca Cozzitorto who from day one of our first meeting has traveled a spiritual journey with me. Together our curiosity and thirst for knowledge gave me the fascinating experience that was written about in this book. I would like to thank my friends Janice (Echoes, Neo-Victorian Poetry) and Emily (Clockwork Twist) Thompson. The writing of this book would not have been possible without your support and encouragement.

Whenever I wanted to give up your kind, wise words lifted me up and kept me going. And I would also like to thank my editor Kelly Cozy (booksidemanner@gmail.com) for all her hard work in making my book perfect. Thank you to Sheena McNeely for her fabulous cover photo and thank you to Torrey Blake for his outstanding computer skills that made it all come together.

Introduction

Arriving a few minutes early for my scheduled appointment, I stood momentarily mystified outside the dark-brown door with the sign: *Hypnosis Clinic. Please Enter.* I was nervous and unsure of what I would experience on the other side of the door; in that moment a struggle began brewing inside me. An anxious, apprehensive interior voice nagged at me, telling me to turn around and go back to the safety of my home. But a much louder voice won out and convinced me to stay and explore the possibilities.

During the twenty-minute drive to my

appointment, I'd had plenty of quiet time to reflect on the events and the soul-searching that had brought me to the door that, once entered, would lead me to a world of the unknown.

It had been thirteen long years since Steve, my hardworking, devoted husband, had died in a tragic automobile accident. It was a loss that had left me psychologically and emotionally damaged. In the months after his death I merely existed, my life a hollow shell. During this time, in addition to the loss of Steve, I also was subjected to several other painful, unfortunate hardships that further damaged my lost and confused spirit.

Performing daily in the greatest acting role of my life, I tried to pretend that I was moving on and healing. But after several years, I finally had to admit to myself that the emotionally resilient, always-cheerful Julie had been actually hiding from everyone, including myself, that I was terribly depressed and trapped by a whirlwind of emotions.

I was seriously in need of professional help to deal with everything that had happened to me over that ill-fated year and a half.

I revealed my almost-unbelievable story to my doctor. He determined that I was suffering from post-traumatic stress disorder (PTSD) and referred me to a PTSD specialist. In six weeks, with the help of some in-depth therapy and antidepressant medication, I was finally starting to feel good and hopeful about life again. In the years following my therapy, I began to reflect deeply on my life, both past and present. I went in search of answers that I hoped would begin to heal my barren and battered soul. I read a multitude of comforting books on the subject of how to cope with the loss of a loved one; these books were quite healing. Living alone gave me the ability to think calmly and at great length about what knowledge I was supposed to have gained from my unexpected experiences. With a new awareness, I began traveling on an enlightened spiritual journey to discover qualities and beliefs within myself that I might not have uncovered had I not experienced some truly life-altering events.

Still harboring some unanswered questions, I started searching deeper for answers. Why did Steve have to die? What happens to our loved ones soul after they die? To find the answers I was seeking, I read more books, this time on the subject of life after death. I choose to read two books that were bestsellers at the time: *Talking to Heaven* by James Van Praagh and *Many Lives, Many Masters* by Brian Weiss. With my newfound knowledge, I found myself seeking out people who had also suffered losses and who were looking for answers. I had deep, thought-provoking conversations with many people who'd had similar experiences, such as my best friend Franca.

Franca and I first met a few months after my husband passed away. We both worked as tellers at a savings and loan. Quickly discovering that we had the loss of a loved one and a need for some deep soul-searching in common, we quickly became fast friends. At the age of thirteen, Franca had lost her father to cancer. It was an emotionally crushing loss that she was still trying to cope with. After this life-altering event she, like me, was left with many unanswered questions.

In what turned out to be a healing form of therapy for both of us, we spent many hours discussing thoughts and feelings about our life experiences and what we perceived might be the meaning of life. During this spiritual exercise I began to believe in a God of my understanding and I began to sense that there was more to life beyond our mere existence. After researching many avenues, Franca and I both found ourselves with a growing interest in reincarnation.

We wondered: What if every person's life was like an imaginatively written book, and each person had a uniquely different story to be told.

Some people might live the exciting life of a riveting epic adventure. Some, sadly, would live a tragic work of literature. Others might be lucky enough to be swept away in a whirlwind of love like that of a romance novel. We began to believe that whatever our own personal story might be, we should embrace it and learn from it, and that we alone have the ability to write the yet-unwritten chapters of our lives — if we choose to do so.

Everyone at one time or another has surely wondered about what happens to us after we die. What happens to our physical bodies is easy to explain. Some are cremated, others are buried. But then what? Do we all just float up to the clouds of Heaven or tumble down to the depths of a fiery Hell? Is that the end of our story? We thought not. God simply had to be more creative than that.

We began to wonder about what happens when we have reached the inevitable final chapter of our life story and the time has come to regretfully close the book of our existence and say, "Is it really, truly over?" Maybe there's more to one's life than meets the eye. Maybe the essence of your being leaves your physical body and travels on to create a continual collection of stories related to your soul's journey of lessons to be learned.

I had long wondered if I had at one time lived another life. Perfect strangers or customers at my job would often say, "Hello, Miss Julie." It seemed natural enough, even though it didn't quite fit in this day and time. When asked why they felt compelled to call me *Miss Julie*, they would reply, "It's because you seem to have a Southern air about you." Their response always seemed odd to me, considering I was born and raised in California. What seemed even stranger was that every so often I would catch myself speaking with a Southern accent and wonder, "Where did that come from?" This occurred so frequently over the years that I began to wonder if it had something to do with a past life, and that perhaps I had once lived in the South.

During this time, both Franca and I had expressed a strong desire to explore our own past lives. Lucky for us, in 2002, the opportunity finally presented itself. While attending San Jose State University, Franca had volunteered to help a professor with a past life regression study. Excited about the possibility of exploring my own past lives, I asked her if he was still looking for volunteers. He was, and I promptly made an appointment for the following week.

That was how I found myself standing outside that office door, filled with curiosity and searching for answers to so many questions. I hoped the hypnosis session I was about to undergo would be able to answer my questions about life and the soul. Was it possible that one's soul continually recreates itself inside another physical body?

As I entered the office, a suspender-wearing, friendly man with thinning gray hair promptly greeted me. The professor introduced himself and explained that he had set up this office for the sole purpose of conducting a study on past life regression. He then led me to a small room, which was cluttered but comfortable. The blinds had been drawn to keep the light at a minimum, and this made the room look even smaller than it already was. The office was equipped with a brown leather recliner, video and audio equipment, and a messy desk piled high with papers. After handing me a pillow and blanket, he asked me to take a seat in the recliner and relax.

He explained that he asked all his participants to take part in one session per week for four weeks, and that a tape of each session would be sent to me within days of our visit. He added that because I had volunteered to assist him in this research he would hypnotize me in a fifth session for whatever reason I would like, such as weight loss or to stop smoking. Once I had agreed to his proposal, he began the session by explaining the lengthy hypnosis process to me.

"3, 2, and 1. Now that you are completely relaxed, focus on the doorway in front of you. On this door hangs a little sign that reads 'time.' Open the door and you'll find stretching before you a long, narrow hallway. The beginning of this hallway is so far ahead of you, so far back in time, that you can't see where it really begins, like railroad tracks that vanish in the distance.

"If you look to the left and right, you will notice little doorways that go off into various different lifetimes along this pathway of your existence. One of those pathways leads to a particular interest to you at this moment, and it will stand out to you in its own way. When you see that door, tell me what it looks like."

There was a long, awkward pause as I searched my mind for any clue of what might be waiting to be revealed. The professor interrupted the silence: "Perhaps what you are seeing is beyond the doorway. You may have gone somewhere already. Some people do. Where are you at this moment?"

With my spellbound mind still unable to conjure up an image, the patient professor continued in vain to help me to visualize anything. Instead of following his instructions, my mind was occupied with the thought that it would help him achieve his objective if I informed him that I didn't feel in any way hypnotized. I heard everything going on around me: the traffic zipping by outside, the people chatting in the office next door. It really didn't feel like anything was different. Thinking that it might be rude to express this when he had already worked so hard to get me to this point, I politely went back to concentrating on what he was saying.

"I'm going to count to three, snap my fingers and see if I can get you moving forward to a different place in time. One, two, three." Snap. "Where are you standing? Are you indoors or out?" he asked. I felt his frustration mounting as he tried in earnest to get me to submit to his guidelines. Not wanting to disappoint, I immersed myself in thought. It took a while, but then I started to see.

The Traveling Circus

Somewhere in the recesses of my mind a distant memory began to take focus. I recognized that I was the rather good-looking young fellow I could see standing beside a large, covered wooden wagon. Not the type of wagon you would have seen on a prairie during the great westward migration, but the type I remember seeing in *The Wizard of Oz*, when the traveling medicine show man was talking to Dorothy. It was rectangular and had big bold letters printed on the side that publicized who we were. The vehicle had been colorfully painted so as to draw attention to it.

The professor asked me if I knew where I was. I told him that I felt I was somewhere in Europe but for some reason I was unable to decipher the time period. If I were to guess, I told the professor, I would probably say somewhere around the early 19th century. The longer I observed the scene, the clearer it was to me that I had been on the move. In fact, I had been traveling great distances with my wife, one oversized elephant, and a substantial group of other people.

I revealed to the professor that I was the proprietor of a small traveling circus, and that my roles were those of the patient and skillful elephant trainer and the attention-grabbing ringmaster. My lovely wife was also my talented assistant, and she was famously known for her agility on the back of our big floppy-eared elephant. The group we traveled with consisted of two humorous and clever clowns, a practiced juggler, the clowns' and juggler's families, and a crew of hardy and efficient helpers.

My wife and I, both in our twenties, were quite comfortable with our nomadic lifestyle, as we shared a similar gypsy heritage. By journeying to the many towns throughout the region, we made our living by performing various well-rehearsed circus acts in front of an excited and inquisitive audience. It was hard to miss us with our horse-drawn caravan of brightly painted wagons of all shapes and sizes, and the huge cage that carried our enormous elephant.

We were unloading our many wagons and soon we would begin preparing for our next show. The small trailer my wife and I shared and called home had just enough room for a built-in bed that could be folded up during the day, and a wooden bench with adequate storage space underneath. Meals that the women prepared and cooked over an open fire pit were served outside. Yearly we made numerous stops on a time-tabled route, so setting up and tearing down our equipment had become second nature to us. For all of us, circus life was what we lived for. No matter how hectic our schedule, we were eager and excited at every stop, and couldn't wait to perform in front of our next group of loyal patrons.

With our whole troupe needing time to train and prepare, we had arrived at our scheduled destination a week early. This additional time helped our naturally gifted elephant Esmeralda adapt to her new environment, and it would afford us the time to adjust our performance based on our new location. Each show we performed had the basic elements, but because this was not our first time performing in this town, we needed to practice to perfection new tricks that would ensure a fresh and exciting show for our many guests.

Only after we felt satisfied that our precious Esmeralda was secure and comfortable in her new location and that we had completed our multitude of necessary tasks for the day, could we settle down for the night. Strategizing around a roaring fire, we would examine carefully every intricate detail of our upcoming show. Under the stars and among the fireflies, our thoughts turned to creating the distinctly different show that we would be performing in a matter of days.

Eagerly our thoughts flowed towards a theme that we hoped would enchant the audience. My wife, with paper and writing implement in hand, readily jotted down each and every one of our expressive ideas, while we were served a simple meal lovingly prepared by the clowns' wives. While we ate, a few of the town's residents dropped by to welcome us, bringing along several bottles of wine. They stayed long into the night, mischievously hoping to uncover what array of surprises we had in store for them this time. Unfortunately for them, we were all tight-lipped and never revealed what we were planning, but they had fun trying to get us drunk enough to tell.

The professor asked me to go back to the

beginning and tell him how this life of adventure and hard work began. Reaching back in my thoughts as far my mind would allow, I began to recount to the professor the earliest part of this life. My wife and I first met at a very young age, when our parents, who were also accomplished performers, began working for the same circus. As a child, I learned the skill of training elephants from my effortlessly talented father. My very supportive mother, not possessing any talent for performing, was perfectly content with collecting the money we earned and handling the bookkeeping for each production.

My wife's family consisted of very well-known acrobats who performed remarkable feats of tumbling, balance, and agility. My wife developed a skill for performing while balanced on the broad back of our elephant; her double back flip was always a crowd pleaser. Inseparable from the very first day we met, we grew up the best of friends. The two of us, preferring to spend all of our time together practicing new performance techniques, had turned into quite a spirited team.

When we reached young adulthood, it didn't take long before our mutually friendly feelings changed into an unending adoration for one another. Finally, we realized what our families had always known: true love was our destiny. With both of us wanting to continue the circus tradition, it became apparent that our real calling was to break away from our families and establish a traveling circus of our own. But first, my love and I were married under the big-top tent in a small ceremony attended by our circus family and close friends.

Weeks later, my wife and I, together with Esmeralda (the young, easygoing elephant my parents had given us as a wedding present) and a few of our close and equally eager friends ambitiously set out to claim our own fame. We traveled south, hundreds of miles away from where we had lived, in order to make a fresh start.

Early on in our journey, without the help and guidance of our families, we struggled to make ends meet. We were stars back home in our circus, but none of that mattered now. Nobody knew us, and nobody cared to learn what our small band of nomads was all about. Unwilling to accept defeat, my wife and I decided to set up our act in a field outside of a well-established town. We then posted hand-drawn, colorful notices around town to let the people know who we were and what talents we had to offer.

In the weeks that followed, we performed our act inside a ring built of logs, whenever a small but appreciative audience would arrive. The always-effervescent Esmeralda, famous for her sweetness, was the highlight of the show. Dressed in her fancy leather-strap headdress with silver studs, she sparkled as she paraded around the ring. On her back rode her pint-sized, energetic, mixed-breed sidekick, darting around in circles while adding a couple of back flips just for the fun of it. I had taught Esmeralda to sit upright on a tiny platform, and while holding a red scarf in her trunk she would enthusiastically wave goodbye at the end of every show to the captivated crowd. With each of our shows so well-received, we felt confident and encouraged that our patrons would return to town with many positive reviews.

As the audiences grew larger, we began taking up collections at the end of each performance from all those who had turned up to be entertained. Before long we had accumulated enough proceeds from our generous spectators to allow us to continue on our journey. Even though we were successful in this small venue, it had become clear that if we were to survive, it was imperative that we expand our show into something more.

Before long we had the good fortune to

encounter three traveling companions; two wildly comical clowns and an amazing, jaw-dropping juggler, all performing their act on the busy streets of a large, well-known city. Viewing their acts, we were enthralled with what we observed. At the end of their spectacular performance we enthusiastically approached the trio and praised them for a job well done. After explaining to them who we were and about our goals, we extended to them a gracious offer to travel and perform with us.

The enchanting trio, being impressed with our circus family history and our strong desire for success, unequivocally agreed to join us. We immediately began planning our new business venture. Coming from backgrounds similar to ours, and carrying with them the same heartfelt passion for our profession, they soon became a part of our circus family.

The two clowns were brothers, but you

wouldn't have been able to tell by looking at them. The older brother was short and stout, with an outgoing personality. The younger one was a quiet, gentle giant. Both of these cleverly talented men had created personas that they had each enhanced with their own unique style.

The shorter, stocky brother wore a costume of long baggy pants held up by a colorful thick rope instead of a belt. He also wore an oversized checkered coat, an overly large polka-dot bow tie, and an old, floppy, weather-beaten hat that covered his curly locks of wild, reddish-orange dyed hair. Heavy white makeup exaggerated his eyes, and his painted-on, cherry-red cheeks completed his jovial look. His act was that of a happy dimwit, which he performed while wearing a comical smile, and his round and animated eyes were laughing and merry. Loudly expressive, with exuberant gestures he had perfected the art of clumsily stumbling and falling down into somersaults so that with each topple the crowd would erupt with laughter.

His taller, younger brother, even with a pathetically slumped posture, still was well over six feet tall. He had succeeded in creating an imaginative identity that was the polar opposite of his much shorter counterpart. He would don a dusty-brown suit that was covered with mismatched patches; this entertaining costume was two sizes too small for his enormous frame. Mounted on top of his disheveled head of hair was a tiny, chestnut-colored bowler hat that was perfect to complete his zany ensemble.

On his face he drew a dark charcoal beard, sloping sad eyes, and exaggerated white lips painted in a downward fashion. His sad and worn-out demeanor made him appear hopeless and down on his luck. His tattered coat, with its many hidden pockets, concealed his magic tricks, and the wilted flower drooping from his lapel completed his sad-sack look.

Unlike his overly chatty brother, he did not speak but instead used practiced routines and body movements to communicate to the crowd. With a tip of his hat, his head drooping with joylessness, he would offer fresh-cut flowers to the ladies sitting in the front rows of the audience. Graciously they thanked him and his discouraged expression turned ever so slightly to hope.

The conservative juggler, described by other circus folk as a bit of an odd character, was set in his ways and hard to please, but his natural artistic inventiveness could not be denied. Skilled in the art of toss juggling and highly experienced at balancing objects, he trained nonstop night and day when he was not performing.

After many years of trial and error he taught himself to juggle flaming wooden pins while balancing a plate of fire on his head. Without fault he could catch objects in flight upon the nape of his neck. To the audience's delight, this self-assured man could also throw a small leather ball out into the crowd, then have them toss it back and with much ease catch it on the end of a stick clenched between his teeth.

Sometimes he would switch up his act by including the always bubbly and vivacious Esmeralda to perform with him. The three of us worked diligently together to perfect a performance in which the smooth-moving juggler would toss Esmeralda bright-colored clubs. Eagerly catching them with her outstretched trunk, Esmeralda would in turn playfully toss them back to the juggler's ready and competent hands.

For his suspenseful grand finale, the shrewd juggler steadied himself on one leg while balancing a ball on the raised foot of the other leg, while at the same time meticulously balancing four porcelain plates on sharp, pointed sticks. This cleverly crafted presentation never failed to receive a standing ovation from the cluster of spellbound onlookers.

All of us had been together as a consummate troupe for some time now. Whether we were meeting new people within the towns and cities we visited or taking in some of Mother Nature's breathtaking scenery, we all felt great delight while traveling on the road. Even though we had ventured through some of the most horrendous weather conditions and driven over some of the worst, bumpiest, most rutted roads ever navigated, our spirits remained high and we never grew tired or bored of each other's company.

Our circus had grown to be quite successful, enough so that it had afforded us some well-deserved comforts. We no longer had to perform our multifaceted presentations outside, where we were often subjected to adverse weather. Now we performed under our own large, canvas, big-top tent while our guests sat on wooden benches.

Our reputation for being captivating entertainers had spread far and wide, so that when we set up in a town or city, large groups of people traveled from miles away just for the joy of being entertained by us. Because of a high demand to see our talent, we now settled in towns for a much longer time and performed several nights a week before returning to the road.

After many years we pretty much knew our route like the backs of our hands. As a matter of course, we traveled by day for as far as we could until sunset each night, when we rested. Slow-moving wagons meant the time traveled between each scheduled town could be as much as a week or more, so to lessen the stress on all of us we planned our shows far in advance.

Each town we visited had its own distinctive ways that cried out for us to notice, and its residents never failed to provide us with a vast array of fresh, raw material. Our troupe members critiqued and shared with each other the defining characteristics and distinctive mannerisms of each town's people, who we watched attentively during our extended stay there. The clowns' insightful ability to mimic our guests was where some of their best material came from. Taking a comical situation that happened in the previous town, the clowns would play it up in the next. Their well-orchestrated performances produced side-splitting laughter.

Because of the nature of our animal act, my wife and I would wait until we had settled into our next location before we could begin practicing. Traveling for long periods could be wearisome; everyone needed time to rest, and elephants were no different. We sought to bestow our loyal companion with all the basic essentials and reassuring comforts we could provide while transporting her from place to place.

Anybody who was familiar with our star

attraction knew there were two sides to this highly spirited elephant. Esmeralda was well known by many for her silly, mischievous nature. Sometimes, when she felt settled and fully rested, her naughty side would emerge. She was notorious for playfully spraying innocent passersby with a trunk full of cold water obtained from her drinking trough, and often left her victims drenched and in disarray.

Then there was Esmeralda's stern and demanding side. All her life Esmeralda had been pampered and overindulged, so much so that she did not take kindly to going unnoticed. While everyone was off readying themselves for the busy day, Esmeralda would raise her wrinkly, stretched-out trunk and trumpet loudly, announcing for all to hear her eagerness to participate. Her noisy, energetic protests could carry on for hours unless I found something for that spoiled princess to do.

Throughout our years of traveling, one particular town had always been a particular favorite of ours. We all seemed unable to resist a certain allure that the charming safe haven exhibited. We were always passionate about performing there and sometimes we willingly remained in that town after our performance ended. Could it have been that the warm feelings bestowed upon us by the welcoming townspeople and the almost perfect weather year-round had created magical powers that kept drawing us back? Even Esmeralda could sense when we were about to return and she simply came alive. The town's harmonious reception always inspired Esmeralda to dedicate her all to every single one of her already heartfelt performances.

Even at the end of our extended stopovers, the delighted patrons beseeched us to remain and perform for them another night or two. The passionate circus lovers took up a collection and feverishly gathered any spare money they had in an attempt to bribe us to stay. Knowing it would be foolish for us to refuse the extra income, we never let on to the townspeople how much this place really meant to us, and we would grant them their wish of a few more days.

Lately, my wife and I had grown weary from our many years on the move, and we discussed the possibility of settling down in the town we had grown to love so much. When we expressed our thoughts to the troupe, the juggler, known for being unreasonable, was adamant that this undertaking would not be in our best interest. Protesting loudly that in order to preserve our name recognition we should remain traveling, he expressed strongly his opinion that the act of settling down was a flawed proposal. The juggler felt that settling in one town would most certainly be our professional demise.

We took into consideration his concerns but we remained hopeful that with some convincing, the clowns and their families would agree with our way of thinking. As time wore on, whenever my wife and I heard the troupe complaining, we would use the opportunity to press our point and slyly pose the question again, just in case any of our stubborn friends had encountered a change of heart.

One year, while ending a stay in a small, unpleasant town that none of us particularly cared for, the physically strong juggler became violently ill. According to the town's doctor, it was not in his best interest to travel for several weeks, so we were required to remain and to tolerate the town's nasty people while he slowly recovered.

The months that followed were very difficult for everyone, as we now had to compensate for the loss of the juggler's act. Even after he was able to perform again, the juggler's prolonged illness kept him from performing at one hundred percent. For more than half the year, our travels from town to town took a heavy toll on him. We knew this willful man was suffering more then he let on, but he always insisted that the show must go on.

By the time we were to perform in our favorite town again, he had physically recovered and was back to his old, fanatical self. The lingering sickness, however, had weakened the juggler's spirit to such a degree that this time, upon our arrival, he confided to us that he would like to discuss settling down and giving our idea of staying in one town a try. My wife and I were quite pleased by this unexpected turn of events. The clowns' and the juggler's families would never do anything without the other, so the three of us pondered how to convince the clowns to go along with the juggler's sudden change of heart.

One evening, the once-inflexible juggler surprised everyone by bringing up the topic of possibly settling in one place. Before anyone had a chance to voice their opinion, the juggler rose up from his chair and, while holding his glass high in the air, prompted us all to lift our glasses and toast to new beginnings. The clowns confessed to my wife and I that they had wanted to settle down years ago, and that all along they had been secretly planting the seed in our pig-headed juggler's mind. It was clear to everyone that the years of constant travel had finally taken a toll on us, and we were all more than ready to have a place to call home.

To our unexpected surprise, the first year had us all, even Esmeralda, feeling restrained and stifled; it was far more difficult than any of us had anticipated. Years of old habits were hard to break. Feeling apprehensive and restless, we never really unpacked. Sensing that we might go, the anxious townsfolk beseeched the town officials to think of something that would entice us to stay.

Fearing the loss of revenue that our thriving circus generated, the town officials offered us the use of an old, abandoned building and its surrounding acreage, located close to the edge of town. We were deeply touched by the kind and generous offer, which would undoubtedly allow us the ability to expand our show and entertain more patrons. Yet still we pondered our choices. The astounding news that my wife was pregnant changed all that for us.

For weeks my weary wife had been having trouble keeping down her breakfast. At first we were unsure if maybe her illness was a contagious stomach ailment, so I isolated her away from our troupe and the rest of the town. The strange and baffling illness came and went throughout the day. When others inquired about her symptoms, she found them unusually difficult to describe. She only knew that it didn't feel like anything she had experienced before and that she just didn't feel well. The other women in our troupe slyly hinted at the possibility that a baby might be on the way. We thought their suggestions impossible, for we had never even discussed the likelihood of having children. My wife and I chose to pay no heed to the women's suggestions.

A few months later, as her belly started to grow, our defiant denials turned into surprised delight. No longer able to ignore the obvious, my wife and I were relieved at our misdiagnosis. There was no denying now that we were going to have a baby and our lives were about to change. All were excited, as this would be the first baby to be born into our circus family in close to a decade. With the fast-spreading news came a joyous celebration thrown on our behalf. As everyone congratulated us, my wife and I knew that our newfound happiness also meant that our contributions to the circus would have to be postponed while we raised the newest member of our family.

No longer able to carry out our circus animal stunts without the talents of my lovely wife, Esmeralda was retrained to be more involved in other acts, leaving me with plenty of spare time. With the help of the townspeople, we immediately went to work renovating the rustic building that had so graciously been given to us. The decaying roof was in bad need of repair, and the inside had to be cleared of useless debris.

Within months the whole building was in tiptop shape. Inside the building we were able to construct a circular arena with strong and secure tiered seating around its edge. Colorful paintings of the clowns performing classic stunts and of the elegant Esmeralda dressed in her finest attire were hung on the walls, bringing our dream closer to fruition. A sense of pride and satisfaction was our reward for all of our hard work and dedication.

When our beautiful baby boy was born, the happiness and delight among our circus group and the townsfolk was more than my wife and I ever expected. Groups of women brought gifts of hand-made baby clothing, and a rocking chair and crib were presented to us by a few of the town's carpenters. All day long, elated groups of spectators gathered in hopes of catching a glimpse of our healthy bundle of love. Many of these curious onlookers openly placed bets on what specific circus role our little boy would have when he grew up.

I listened proudly as some folks bet that he would inherently take after me and not only train elephants, but extend the act to include other animals as well. The comical clowns and the steadfast juggler were hoping he would grow up to admire their talents enough to develop a passion to follow in their footsteps. All this interest in our son's future was highly flattering, but we would just have to patiently wait for the events that had yet to come.

Two years later the same bets were made about our adorable baby girl. Although most people bet that she would take after her nimble, acrobatic mother, others wanted her to have a wealth of opportunities and to not be limited by her gender.

As she grew into a toddler, it was obvious to everyone how much she adored Esmeralda and our daily visits with the elephant. When my little precious one cried out for me to lift her, I would gently position her on the curl of Esmeralda's broad, inviting trunk. As my daughter hugged the trunk tightly, Esmeralda would then playfully swing her from side to side, soothing my darling daughter with her gentle motions. Attentive circus hands, viewing our playful ritual, placed bets on our little girl, not my son, to be the one destined to be an accomplished elephant trainer. Further fueling the speculations was the fact that everywhere I went, throughout the day my little sidekick stuck to me like glue. Yes she was daddy's little girl. We did everything together — that is, until she turned six.

In the years following the birth of our two children, there had been many thrilling new additions to our circus family. Traveling acts returned to perform with us every year, and many made the decision to settle down just as we had. The first to make such a decision was a family of brilliant trapeze performers that my wife and I had befriended. About our age, with the same desire for perfection, they quickly became part of our well-established show.

Our son and daughter, now eight and six years old respectively, were mesmerized by the trapeze performers' remarkable skills, which required them to have precise timing and a great deal of strength, grace, and flexibility. The children, completely captivated by the troupe's aerial entertainment, spent most of their waking hours observing these courageous artists as they gracefully trained high above the arena floor.

While I witnessed my children's transfixed expressions of awe, mixed emotions ran rampant through my mind, heart, and soul. On one hand, I was deeply saddened by the loss of their attention, especially from daddy's little girl, and my heart ached with loneliness because my cherished children were involved in the lives of the flying trapeze family rather than with us. Yet I also felt pleased and grateful that my highly motivated children were displaying an interest and passion for performing the arts, even though I secretly wished that their desire and enthusiasm were to take after mine.

The professor asked me to move ahead in time.

I told him that my children, now about the same age that my wife and I had been when we started performing together, had through long, rigorous hours of training become quite a dynamic duo in the art of the flying trapeze. They jumped from the narrow pedestal board, allowing gravity to create a pendulum sway, and performed mid-air somersaults at the peak of the swing. The first time I saw my boy swing, release the bar, fly through the air while tumbling head over heels and then grab on to a second bar, I felt a rush of excitement.

At times my strong, athletic son also performed the role of unwavering catcher and assistant to my daughter. Hanging by his knees with his legs tightly wrapped around the ropes of the horizontal bar allowed my son to dangle perilously upside down, holding his suspended sister with one hand as she bent her fit and flexible body in unbelievable ways. From below, my wife and I watched as they performed gracefully expressive movements with intense exhilaration and our talented children's performance made us feel unbelievably proud.

Because of their passion and practice, as my children matured, their dream to become the most well-known flying trapeze act ever came to fruition, when they were able to perfect the most exceptional, dynamic, awe-inspiring movements ever performed.

Over the years they extended the act to include ropes and rings, and my daughter added her ability to rapidly spin by a metal bit she clenched in her teeth. My children continued to work as an unstoppable team throughout the years. As for all those bets placed by our troupe when they were first born? Well, no one ended up winning that wager.

As my wife and I aged, we slowly stepped out of the spotlight. Our transition into retirement was easy as our children effortlessly took center stage. The clowns and juggler had long since departed from this life and it had been noticeable for some time that Esmeralda herself was way past her prime as she missed her cues and was often not responsive to my commands. It saddened me to watch my once-vibrant elephant struggle to perform. My wife and I, after years of worrisome soul-searching, heartbreakingly decided that Esmeralda, our steadfast companion for decades, would have to be put down as she was no longer able to earn her keep.

As I told the note-writing professor about my long, well-lived life, I said I felt fortunate to have had only great memories and no regrets. Traveling and performing had been an essential part of my being, but I was fully aware that without the love of my devoted wife, my adoring children, and my beloved elephant, all of whom spent many years by my side, my heart would not have carried the fulfilled contentment it possessed. God had truly blessed me with a good life.

As I heard the professor's voice telling me that it was time to move on from that life, I told him how humorous I thought it was that I had lived the life of a circus performer and how ironic it was, because in my current life I wasn't particularly fond of the circus. Quickly changing the subject, he urged me to search my mind for the next vision

Civil War, Georgia

To my amazement, the next scene began to materialize rather quickly, as if it was impatiently waiting to be known. I visualized an attractive teenage girl with long, lush auburn hair standing in the heart of a grassy meadow, and I knew that the pretty young girl was me. I found myself looking at a vast wooded countryside with rolling hills and far-off mountain peaks, and I sensed the warmth of the afternoon sun.

A flood of thoughts entered my mind, enlightening me to the fact that I was here on an outing with a few of my classmates from school.

We had come here to collect a variety of bugs and butterflies for a nature project we had due next week. Cleverly, we had chosen just the right spot along a wandering creek where there were an abundance of perfect specimens for us to observe.

The sound of turning wheels and the clatter of pounding hoofs suddenly interrupted my peaceful surroundings. In the distance, I caught sight of my mother and father traveling down the bumpy dirt road in a horse-drawn carriage. As I watched them approaching an old, covered bridge it occurred to me that they had arrived to take me home. I explained to the professor that I felt we were having an important dinner party at our house that night, and that I must return home to dress for the evening's festivities.

After a short ride down a well-traveled, two-lane dirt road, my father turned onto a lengthy driveway that was lavishly shaded by a canopy of giant oak trees. This impressive private road led to a large estate where our stately, two-story, Colonial-style house with its white pillars, shuttered windows, and a spacious covered porch, awaited us.

As the carriage slowed to a halt in front of our house, out of nowhere a little dog scampered to greet me with his long turned-up tail wagging with excitement. Corky, a white terrier with black spots and a wiry coat, was well known around these parts for his enthusiastic energy and his irresistible personality.

My focus veered away from Corky, who was now perched in my lap, as I caught sight of Miles, one of our servants, walking towards the carriage to greet us. His tall, strong frame was quite striking, and he carried himself with ease. As usual, he was there to help me and my mother climb down from the carriage. I expressed to the professor that Miles was a very kind and gentle man, whom I liked very much, and that I considered him to be part of our family.

I further explained to the professor that for as far back as I could recall, Miles had been my family's loyal servant and had tended to my every need. I recalled how when I was a little girl I treasured the special moments I had with Miles — especially when he would gently lift me up onto his lap with his big, strong arms, and tell me captivating stories about what it was like growing up when he was a little boy.

At times, I had felt closer to a number of our servants than I had to my own family. My mother, a stern disciplinarian, expected nothing but the best out of me at all times. I got along best with my Daddy, but unfortunately for me, he was a busy man. Deprived of spending any quality time with him, I genuinely craved his attention.

Because of my parents' active commitment to the political and economic life of the South, it was the servants' responsibility to care for me in my parents' absence. Curious, I often made inquiries about how those hard-working subordinates accomplished their daily household tasks. Unlike my mother, who found me to be a bit of a nuisance at times, the servants had the tolerance needed to teach me their domestic chores. I learned about cooking and sewing, tasks I would never personally have to do, but it was fun learning about what the servants did on a daily basis. Their methods of preparing the ground and sowing the rice out in the fields were also fascinating. All of this, however, did not please my mother. She felt that learning such things was beneath me and that this was not at all how a young lady of the house should behave.

At that point in the hypnosis session, the professor asked me what my name was. In a self-assured Southern accent I proclaimed, "I am Miss Annabelle Conner. I am seventeen years old and I live in the grand state of Georgia." He asked if I knew the name of the town I was from but I had trouble recalling its name.

I told him that my Daddy spoiled me and called me "princess." I also stated matter-of-factly that I was very pretty and boys liked me. I had a habit of bragging about myself, and spoke at great length about how everyone I knew admired and complimented me on the beautiful, long, auburn hair that gracefully flowed over my shoulders and stopped midway down my back.

The party we were hosting that night was a celebration. The Southern states had recently united for a cause they truly believed in, and were now anticipating going to war against the Northern states. My father, who I now realized to be some sort of a political figure, would be giving a very important speech pertaining to this matter.

For this rare and historic occasion, we were expecting most of the townspeople to turn out at our home. My father said everyone he had talked to was elated about the coming war, and there was no doubt that victory would be ours. I had heard my father declare that the time had finally arrived for us to fight to preserve our way of life. All those attending tonight were in accord with my father's way of thinking.

Well, almost all those attending. My feelings about the situation were very different from those of my parents. I was not at all excited about the passionate men and boys of our glorious state going to fight in some silly war. Was violence and killing the only way to solve our differences? I liked my life just the way it was and I stubbornly refused to understand why things had to change. Nonetheless, I was expected to dress up, behave like a young lady, and in no way express my opinion on the matter.

Because I despised dressing up, my methodical mother was often annoyed with me. As her reluctantly obedient daughter, I was constantly reminded that I was expected to look my best at all social functions. Honestly, I was a bit of a tomboy, and if I'd a choice, I would rather have been outside climbing a tree or playing with my dog, than attending some boring old party.

However, since I was required to attend and be gracious, I had chosen to wear my favorite cornflower-blue dress — the one my Daddy so adored. The off-the-shoulder neckline connected to short puffy sleeves, beautiful lace adorned the bottom of the flowing skirt, and a big white bow cascaded down the back of the dress, extending almost to the floor. If I looked my prettiest, there would be something I could be happy about tonight.

The ever-painful corset ritual that my mother insisted on performing was the thing that I loathed most about dressing up. Showing no pity for the pain I was about to endure, my mother squeezed me so tightly into my corset that it was almost impossible for me to breathe and I was sometimes brought to tears. By the time my mother was done pulling and tugging, my waist was close to disappearing. She stepped back and admired her accomplishment with a proud, victorious smile.

My mother, wasting no time, was now on to the final touches. Once I'd slipped into my dress, my hair was combed to perfection. I couldn't help but stare at my flawless reflection in the mirror, all the while singing my own praises about how beautiful I was. My mother, shaking her head, chided me for being so vain. "I'm not the only one who thinks that, Mother," I snapped, "Daddy was sure to tell me that he thinks I look pretty, too."

Pausing at the top of the staircase before I made my poised and dignified descent, I prayed a certain boy I had a crush on would be among the uniformed soldiers arriving downstairs. Never before had he had the opportunity to see me as strikingly impressive as I was this evening. I would find myself extremely disappointed if he was not downstairs among the attendees.

The only drawback my beauty caused me was that it made my Daddy very strict and overbearing, especially when it came to the boys I knew. Even through I was old enough to be courted, he never allowed young men my age to come calling. Recently he had become angered that I liked this one particular boy, probably because he knew the boy was a few years older than me. Sneaking off to meet him whenever I was in town was the only way we could spend time together.

At this point in the session, a sudden realization came over me. I told the professor I sensed my Civil War parents were also my parents in my current life, and I could see a few parallels between the relationships in both lives. My mother in my current life was also the disciplinarian and my father, the one I got along with best, worked long hours so I didn't get to spend much time with him either. I also noticed that in both lives my beliefs differed from those of my parents. In my current life my parents and I disagreed about religion; in Annabelle's life, it was about war. In both lives, the disagreements did not please my parents much.

As I descended our long, grand staircase, my eyes eagerly scanned the crowd of guests mingling in the foyer. Two uniformed soldiers standing at attention by the entrance, each one holding a rifle with a bayonet attached, immediately caught my eye. But alas, they were not whom I was looking for. Making my way through the tightly packed crowd, I was surprised by the unusual number of Army officers in attendance, wearing their gray dress uniforms adorned with shiny gold buttons.

I continued searching in earnest for the young soldier I had a fondness for, but to my disappointment he was not there. I suspected that my possessive father had suggested to the commanding officer that my soldier not be present this evening. In addition to that huge disappointment, I noticed not a single one of my friends was present either. Now this evening's event was going to be much more painful and tedious than I had originally anticipated.

I meandered through our crowded house, which was alive with the chatter of our many guests. All present were anxious to hear my father speak. As he summoned everyone to assemble in the parlor, my mother and I proudly took our places beside him. I listened as my father started his speech by stating what he believed in his heart to be true, that the time had come for the dedicated South to stand up and fight. He informed the guests that Georgia and several other Southern states had declared their secession from the United States and had already established an alliance of states called the Confederacy.

He maintained that the newly formed Confederacy was angry with the recently elected president of the United States, Mr. Abraham Lincoln, for not wanting to expand slavery beyond the states in which it already existed. My father said if this was allowed to happen, slavery would surely die and this would devastate our economy. I was suddenly taken aback when my father shouted, "The people of the South have no other choice; we must fight to preserve our beliefs and traditions we have long held."

Judging by the reactions on the intense faces before me, I could tell that my father's fiery, passionate speech was having a profound effect. Cheers of approval and loud outbursts of encouragement seemed to further fuel my father's loyalty to the South. I, on the other hand, had grown terribly bored and wished this whole dreary evening would end sooner rather than later.

Once my father's speech had ended it was

far too warm to remain inside, so we all slowly made our way out onto the covered porch to enjoy the evening meal. The servants had worked diligently, since the crack of dawn, to prepare for us savory veal pie and chicken croquettes, refreshing dressed cucumbers with chilled sliced tomatoes, rice with black-eyed peas, honey corn bread made just the way I liked it, and peach ice cream for dessert. To drink, our quests were served queen's punch and some cool and refreshing mint juleps. I enjoyed the punch, but found it a bit challenging to eat any of the delicious food with my stubborn corset being so unbearably tight.

After dinner had ended, I became bored rather quickly. Secretively I tiptoed upstairs to write in my journal about the highlights of this long, exhausting day. With all that had transpired — my classroom field trip, my father's talk of war, the absence of my soldier friend — I surely had a lot to write about. Because my parents forbade me to air my personal opinions in public, I had no choice but to let out my feelings in my journal. Unfortunately, my vigilant mother detected my absence quickly and called me to return back downstairs.

The professor asked me to skip ahead a few years and relay to him what I visualized next.

What my mind revealed next were feelings of much urgency. My intensely anxious parents and I were rapidly traveling down the carriageway that would lead us into town, and more specifically to the town hall. It had become imperative that my father summon the townsfolk together to discuss the tragic turn this horrific war had taken and what, if anything, we could do to save our town from the death and destruction heading its way.

We sat in stunned silence as we passed once-stately homes that had been burned and plundered by the aggressive Northern armies. Because we lived outside of town, we had been spared these mean and senseless acts; I closed my eyes and took a brief moment to thank God for this.

The sight of our once-scenic countryside now ravaged by war left us stunned. My feelings were very different from the excitement everyone had felt a few years back at that celebration; what I felt now was deep despair. This war was not at all what my father had envisioned it would be. What was once deemed to be a noble fight and an easy, victorious win had evolved into unnecessary loss and devastation.

While traversing through the crowded streets towards our destination, I became extremely confused as, for the first time, I witnessed our beaten-down and disillusioned soldiers struggling to make their way through town, bandaged and bloody. I gasped, "Oh dear God" as I pointed out to my parents some men who were missing arms and legs. My father slowed down to let pass a band of exhausted soldiers, who pushed their heavy bronze cannons mounted on wooden carriages with what little strength they had left.

I was stunned to realize that I could clearly see the distraught expressions etched upon these poor soldiers' wretched and emaciated faces. Suddenly I caught a whiff of a horrendous stench unlike anything I had ever smelled before. It was the smell of death in the stagnant air, coming from an approaching flatbed wagon stacked full with the rotting corpses of our ill-fated soldiers. I couldn't help but wonder why it had come to this. What point did all this suffering and destruction serve?

Although my father had come to town in a last-ditch effort to alert the citizens of the rapidly approaching danger, it was really no surprise to anyone still living there. Being on the losing end of the war had already created a town in mourning. Frequently, the townsfolk could hear nearby cannons firing. It gave them little hope of ever again leading the lives that they had been so accustomed to living. Before reaching the town hall, my father made my mother and I vow to not reveal to anyone the devastation we had witnessed on our ride into town. He said, "It would serve no purpose."

Secretly, my well-informed parents had been worried for some time about our soldiers' inability to hold back the advancing Union army. I had overheard them discussing whether or not we should pack up and flee to a safer location, but both of them knew down deep in their hearts that they could not abandon the town they had loved so dearly.

As we swiftly entered the hall, off to my right was a small gathering of sobbing women who had just read a newly posted list of casualties and learned about the deaths of their loved ones. Stunned and dazed by all the unfolding events, unsure of what my role should be, I stood frozen as my compassionate mother tried in vain to console each and every one of them.

It was beyond belief how many of our town's men had died tragic deaths so far. In this latest bloody battle it was reported that over twenty-three thousand men had perished. No one was spared, not the fathers, not the husbands, and the most heartbreaking of all, not the young boys who were just beginning their lives, their potential unfulfilled.

I watched as my brave father regretfully took to the podium. Looking out upon the distressed faces of those seated before him, mostly women and young children, it became apparent to him that his town had already been defeated. He had been stubbornly living in denial, but now the reality of what this merciless war really meant was seated right before him. He had finally realized that the celebrated South the people of this town once knew had been lost to them forever. Overcome by raw emotion, my father simply bowed his head in sadness. There was nothing left for him to say.

Again the professor told me to skip ahead.

When the news first reached us that President Lincoln had signed the Emancipation Proclamation, an executive order to free all slaves, there was much rejoicing within the slave quarters. Their songs of joy echoed through the air and could be heard by us up in the main house. My parents knew those sounds meant the last piece of our Southern heritage was about to be stripped away. For my father, this wasn't just a slap in the face but a deepening of the wounds that had already been inflicted. Our slaves' release was not immediate, but we knew it was just a matter of time before freedom came knocking.

When the day finally came for Miles to set out for a new life of independence, he solemnly took me aside. His voice wavered with emotion as he said how truly regretful he was that after all his years of endless devotion he was about to abandon me. He wanted me to understand that his leaving was not in any way meant to hurt me. It was something he had to do courageously for himself and his family, and he hoped that one day I would grasp its true meaning. With that said, he ended our mutual bond by embracing me with a long, heartfelt goodbye.

Turning away from me, he slowly bent down, picked up his belongings and without ever looking back, sauntered away with his head held high. Miles was now a proud man, a free man. Overwhelmed by extreme sorrow, I was at a loss for words and my eyes overflowed with tears. Feelings of abandonment coursed through me as I watched my beloved Miles and the few slaves that were left exit our property onto the road towards freedom, and out of my life.

It had been well over four long, heartrending years since the fateful decision was made to go to war. And now I had lost everything. My parents, once known for their passionate interest in life, were just shadows of their former selves. Believing that I was the only reason they had to keep living, I tried in vain to bring normalcy to their lives, but I too was deeply depressed. All of the pretty things that I used to take for granted had either been stolen or sold, and now I'd just lost my best friend and confidante Miles. Never again did I see that kind and caring man.

Six years passed. I was twenty-five years old now and the long ruthless war had been over for some time. Contentment and prosperity, once shared by the people of our town, were stolen by the conflict and had not returned. The soulless war that had marauded through the South had also robbed the town of so many of its eligible men; I was now considered an old maid.

A few years back, I'd heard that the young soldier I'd had a crush on had died a lonely death along the banks of the Chattahoochee River, not far away. When I heard the news, though I tried, I could not muster up any feelings of sadness for my old friend. I wanted desperately to care about his passing, but the years of war had rendered me incapable of compassion.

My father, once a strong and confident man, was now just an empty shell after years of struggle. For some reason he blamed himself for the death and destruction the war had brought to his town and its people. I watched him with much despair as day after day he sat on the porch, slumped in his old rocking chair, and stared vacantly out over the ruins of his once-productive plantation. He pondered if there was something he could have done to make the outcome of the war different. Over and over again, he questioned every decision he'd made prior to the South going to war, but the answers cruelly escaped him.

Wearing the look of a forgotten man, my

languishing father continually punished himself. This self-imposed life sentence weighed heavily upon his shoulders and left me troubled and concerned about his declining health.

During the war my father failed at his valiant efforts to preserve our more-than-adequate bank holdings. We no longer possessed the wealth we once had and every day was an agonizing struggle to survive. Our once magnificent home had become run-down and badly needed repair. Gone were the glory days when our house was alive with the hustle and bustle of daily activities. These days, our house stood eerily quiet. Often the only sound that could be heard was that of the cruel gnawing wind as it howled its way through the many cracks in our creaking walls.

By the time I was thirty-five, both of my parents had died, most certainly in part to hunger and the heartbreak they'd endured since the war began. I alone cared for them until they died, and with the help of a neighbor I buried them behind the home they had so loved. A plain wooden cross was all I had to mark their grave.

I lived all alone in my big, dilapidated house; anybody I had ever known had long forsaken me. Now I sat and wondered: if I had been more kind and polite growing up, perhaps I would not be alone now. Desperate and depressed, I spent most nights upstairs in the safe haven of my bedroom where I found some comfort in my old journals. Reading through the many pages I had written while I was growing up, I fondly remembered the time before the war and how privileged and comfortable my life had been. As I continued to read the sometimes thoughtless words the selfish girl I had once been had written, I wished I would have appreciated all my parents had given me.

Too proud to seek out help, I spent most of my lonely days foraging for whatever small amounts of fruit, rice, or anything else I could find to eat. My cold, skinny body ached from lack of nourishment and my once-admired beauty had disappeared along with all the people I had known. Feelings of hopelessness consumed me and I was so depressed that I didn't care to live like this anymore. Daily I prayed to God to let me die so that I might be reunited with my mother and father again.

At this point, the professor sympathetically asked me to skip ahead to the time of my death and to share the experience with him.

After years of slow starvation, death finally came at the age of forty-two. From my bed, my now-peaceful soul ascended, abandoning what remained of my thin and wasted body. Taking with me my thoughts and perceptions, I floated upward towards the bright light that beckoned me. I felt joy and relief to be leaving that miserable existence behind. All at once a feeling of tranquility rushed through me as I entered into the warmth of the light. For a moment I was blinded by its pure illumination, and then slowly a colorful scene began to appear before me.

I stood in a beautiful garden where unexpectedly I caught sight of my Daddy with his loving arms stretched open wide. Without hesitation I darted jubilantly towards his welcoming gesture and he embraced me with the most welcoming hug I'd had in a very long time. For years I had prayed for God to allow this day to happen, and now I felt elated and blessed to be finally reunited with him. Basking in the comfort of my father's strong arms, I heard approaching from behind me the sounds of a familiar bark. As I turned, much to my surprise I saw my little dog Corky running to greet me with his bony little tail wagging with joy, just like it did on the day of the celebration.

As I bent down to pet his wiggling little body, I noticed off in the distance my angelic mother standing in the midst of a sea of soldiers. Staring into their many faces, I noticed that the tired and hungry looks that had been etched in my memory for so many years were no longer present. Thankfully, these soldiers were finally at peace.

Taking my hand, my Daddy and I began to walk in silence along a babbling brook that wound its way through the peaceful garden. The stream itself was breathtakingly beautiful and the sound of water rushing over the rocks was soothing to me. My father guided me to a still pool of water where I caught a glimpse of my reflection. I was taken aback to discover that I was no longer the skinny and sickly woman I had been before arriving at this heavenly place. Instead I looked young and pretty again.

The sudden distant laughter of children drew my attention away from my reflection and I looked up to see them chasing after a big, red ball. It had been a long time since I had heard the joyous sounds of laughter, and it brought a carefree smile to my face. Watching them, I somehow got caught up in their happiness and I found myself belting out the loudest laugh I had ever had. The contentment I felt in that moment made me want to remain in that blissful place forever.

But it was not to be.

Without warning, I felt myself in free fall, unable to control my destination and uncertain of what awaited me next.

.

1930s New York

After the tranquility of the mystical garden, the free fall I found myself in felt like I would imagine it would feel if I had just jumped out of a plane without a parachute. But after crossing the threshold into a new life, that feeling of free fall was replaced with an incredible sense of warmth and tranquility. I seemed to be completely enclosed and it was difficult to perceive anything in the darkness that surrounded me. Wherever I was, I felt safe and protected. So rather then question the situation, I decided to relax and immerse myself in the experience.

The warm, encompassing place I inhabited was stress-free and comfortable. But without any warning, I felt myself being pushed through some kind of narrow passageway that felt slimy and gooey. This sensation was very strange and also intimidating, as I was not in control of what was happening to me. Then I realized this was the moment I had been waiting for; that push was my cue to be born. "I'm stuck, no, wait. Whoa, it's bright out here!" I thought upon my arrival into this new life.

The next things I experienced were being turned upside down and suddenly given a sharp slap on my butt. The shock of that slap did not make me happy and I immediately burst out into a loud cry. The doctor then gently handed me to my mother's waiting arms. Looking up, while nestled against her warm and comforting chest, I saw her welcoming smile and loving eyes staring back at me. The soft rhythm of her heartbeat sent me signals of love.

The professor asked me to move ahead a few years and to tell him more about this life.

I told him, "My name Kathy and I am seven years old."

"What are you doing right now, Kathy?" he asked.

I was sitting outside on the steps of the apartment house where I lived, and I was furious. My stubborn Mom refused to let me play ball out in the street with my older brother and sister. She treated me like I was a baby because she had some weird fear that playing in the streets would not be safe for me.

For as far back as I could remember it had been the same thing every day. After school and on weekends, my brother and sister were allowed to go out and have the best time of their lives, playing kickball with all the other neighborhood kids, while I had to sit on the stairs and watch. With each passing day I grew more and more angry and longed for the day when I, too, would be old enough to join in all the fun and games.

I told the professor I saw long rows of apartments with stairways leading from the sidewalk up to second-floor entrances. The buildings were located in a very hectic part of the city and the apartments looked like the brownstone housing they have in the northeast. From my perch at the top of the stairs I could see numerous parked cars lining the streets, and I became aware of a tremendous amount of horn-honking traffic. I also observed several city sidewalks that were crowded with people hurriedly walking to their destinations. Looking up, I could see that the apartments on our block were surrounded by many significantly taller buildings. In fact, the buildings were so tall that they blocked out the noonday sun. The professor interrupted me to ask if I knew the name of the city I was describing. I replied, "It's called New York."

I complained to the professor that the gray cement steps outside our brownstone were my prison and that I was destined to remain in this spot and never to play or have fun. Apparently, I was not old enough to play in the street, though I knew for a fact that one of the neighborhood kids was younger than me. This girl was only six, but her carefree mother let her play out there whenever she wanted.

With every laugh and scream I heard, I imagined the other kids were taunting me.

It just was not fair and I didn't understand why my mom was punishing me. Bound and determined, I made a promise to myself that one of these days I was going to play like all the other kids. For months I had secretly planned my escape from that Brownstone Step Prison.

My dutiful Mom, along with most of the other hard-working women in our neighborhood, worked at the local laundry, one of the biggest in town. Regardless of health or weather, six mornings a week she would rise early and resignedly walk the eight blocks to her job. The laundry, located in a large, twelve-story, red brick building, had a multitude of windows on each floor that opened out towards the street.

On the ninth floor, where my mom worked, red-faced women standing on both sides of long metal tables vigorously ironed. They used heavy steam irons attached to long cords that ran along wires that draped across the room. The room's thick, stagnant air was so uncomfortably hot and stuffy that the windows remained open for most of the year, except in the dead of winter. I had gone with my mother to her job enough times to know that the laundry was not the kind of place I wanted to work in when I grew up.

My mother was unnaturally thin for her height and she was always exhausted when she arrived home late at night. She struggled weekly to make ends meet and despite the brutally long hours she worked, we were always short on money. Our clothes were hand-me-downs and most weeks it was watered-down soup and stale bread for our nightly supper. She would incessantly tell us that there was no need to worry, and reassured us with her favorite saying: "With the good Lord's help, I'll manage somehow to get us through another month."

At that point in the session, my mother's financial struggles alerted me to the fact that I had no recollection of ever having had a father in this life. I told the professor that I was not sure what the story was with him, since no mention of him had been made so far, but I did perceive he had been absent from our lives for some time.

Because my mother was the sole provider for the four of us, my conscientious fourteen-year-old brother had taken it upon himself to lessen my mother's burden by stepping up to be the man of the family. For the past two years, he'd worked tirelessly as a paperboy to help our Mom pay the rent and keep food on the table.

Every morning, like clockwork, my brother rose before dawn to deliver his fresh- off-the-press newspapers throughout the surrounding neighborhoods on his old, poorly- rebuilt bike. Most mornings he was back home in time to have a quick breakfast with my sister and me before we were all off to school.

Once a month, after collecting his paper route money, my brother emptied his pockets and dumped his earnings onto the kitchen table. With anxious anticipation, my mother quickly counted up the money while my brother hurried off to start his homework. Depending on the amount he received from his tips, my Mom either smiled and was pleased with the money, or a worried look crept across her face. Her concerned look was always a sign that it would be necessary for her to work long, back-breaking hours again that month.

My devoted brother was never one to complain and seemed comforted by his responsibilities. He seemed to attain pleasure from helping our mother provide for us. My caring and thoughtful brother often sat with me on my prison steps to help ward off any feelings of loneliness I had.

My twelve-year-old sister, on the other hand, was nothing more than a big pain in the butt. She was overly obsessed with boys and wasn't much help around the house. All she ever wanted to talk about were the boys at school, the boys in the neighborhood, boys, boys, and boys. I just didn't get it; to me they were all mean and creepy. My sister would constantly tell me that someday when I was older I would like them too, but I was pretty certain that was never going to happen.

Living directly across the hall from us was a kindhearted older couple. They caringly looked after the three of us a few hours each weekday evening and on Saturdays while our mother was still at work. Acting as surrogate grandparents, this childless couple had been a blessing in our mother's life, helping to ease some of her worries and nerve-racking responsibilities. On a number of occasions, when my mother was working later then usual, they would help her by feeding us a full and satisfying dinner. My mother, a proud woman, would offer them money for their kindness but they would always refuse her payment.

When it was time for us to arrive home from school, the good-natured woman was usually standing at the top of the stairs, patiently awaiting our return and ready to greet us with a big, welcoming smile. From halfway down the street we could see the red-and-white-checked apron she sometimes wore, and that almost always meant she would be holding a plate of something yummy she had baked for us that day.

Her suspender-wearing husband and my brother, who were both big Yankee fans, would spend hours talking about their love of baseball and the players on the team. They expressed excitement for some new guy named Joe DiMaggio and all the home runs he had batted during the 1936 season, and they shared their mutual disappointment when a player named Babe Ruth (a funny name for a man) left a few years back to play for another team. The closest person my brother ever had to a father figure, this thoughtful man promised to try to obtain a couple of hard-to-come-by tickets so the two of them could attend a Yankees game, which had always been a huge fantasy of my brother's.

While the two of them jabbered on about guy stuff, his wife found pleasure in teaching my sister and me her craft of knitting. As a Christmas surprise for our mother, we were knitting soft, warm blankets for each of our beds and we were delighted with our progress so far. My siblings and I were fully aware of how lucky we were to have these thoughtful, generous people in our lives and we were truly grateful for our time spent together. Each night before bed, we willingly included them in our nightly prayers and asked God to please bestow His kindness on them.

One day I felt strong and defiant, and decided that today was the day. All of the parts to my plan seemed to be lined up perfectly. My unsuspecting Mom was in the house washing dishes, my protective brother and tattling sister were nowhere close by, and the neighborhood kids were having their usual fun playing out in the street. As part of my secret plot, I took a seat on our brownstone steps while holding a book I pretended to read. Really, I was just waiting for the right moment to make my break from this prison and run out into the street to play with the other kids, even if it was just for a moment.

Certain that every aspect of my plan was

just right, I made a break for it, running full speed ahead towards the happy kids playing kickball. When I got about two-thirds of the way there, I glanced back to make sure my Mom wasn't looking, and out of the blue I felt myself floating up above the other children, who had suddenly stopped playing. Hovering above the scene, I looked down at the kids and saw that they were now running towards the car that had come to a screeching halt in the middle of the street.

To my surprise, I could see a small figure lying on the pavement with the car almost on top of it. As I took a closer look I noticed that it was a little girl wearing the exact same outfit I wore. She had on a little worn-out pink skirt with ruffles at the bottom and a matching short-sleeve, pink-and-white polka-dot top. I noticed that she was not moving and that the driver of the car was trying to wake her.

Around the tragic scene, a small crowd had

begun to form. Glancing over at the brownstone I could see that my mother was now running from the house. With her hair in curlers, her apron still on, and a dishtowel in hand, she was frantically screaming at the top of her lungs and heading straight for the motionless little girl in the middle of the street. Taking a closer look at the confusing scene below, I instantly realized that the poor little motionless girl was actually me.

I was stunned. What I had thought would be a crafty way for me to escape from my brownstone prison steps turned out to be not so clever after all. Stupid, stupid me. My sensible mother was right; I should have listened to her. Today was supposed to be the day that I finally had the fun that I had longed for, not to depart from this life at the young age of eight.

I continued to watch as the chaos unfolded below me. My hysterical mother had wormed her way through the mounting crowd of bystanders and was now bent over my lifeless body, sobbing hysterically. Even though I knew that it was me lying down there, I couldn't help but think, "Poor little girl."

In the distance, wailing sirens could be heard, desperately making their way through the crowded streets. My brother and sister had just arrived and they knelt next to my mother, holding her in their arms. Having a compassionate urge to do something as I observed my brother and sister trying their best to console her, I said loudly, "Don't cry, Mama." But she was too sad to hear me.

In the blink of an eye, I found myself rising higher than I had ever been, until I could no longer make out the poignant images below. I found myself back in the serenity of the beautiful garden that I had visited before. Off in the distance I could see the blurred image of a man approaching me with open arms. As he drew nearer, it became clear to me that this smiling man was my Civil War

Daddy coming to welcome me back. His inviting gesture filled me with joyfulness and I ran eagerly into his loving embrace. The happiness I felt from yet again reuniting with this adoring man who had once meant so much to me was more than I could express.

With what I thought was poor timing, the professor announced, "This will be all for today. Let's have you return to your present lifetime." With a one, two, three, snap he brought me back. As I opened my heavy, glazed-over eyes I was surprised and slightly taken aback by what I had just experienced.

I told the professor that the entire experience felt as if I had been daydreaming and now that I was back it felt as if I had just returned from some kind of strange time warp. He gave me an understanding nod and I got the feeling that it was not the first time he had heard those words. I glanced down at my watch and was surprised to learn that my spellbinding session had lasted over three hours. I could have sworn no more than an hour had passed, but it would make sense that going through the hypnosis process and recalling three lives would have taken much longer. The whole thing felt so surreal.

The professor was still jotting down notes when I offered up one of the main reasons I had volunteered to participate in this past life study. I told him I wanted to solve a puzzling mystery I'd encountered in my daily life. I told him all my life I had thought I had lived a life in the South. The professor let out a slight chuckle as he said, "Well, Julie, it looks like you solved your mystery. You were once a Georgia peach."

As the professor and I reflected back on my Civil War life, I began to see some similarities between my current life and those of my past lives. I told the professor that Annabelle and I had shared some similar values. Even though Annabelle was the daughter of a slave owner, she did not share the same prejudices as her peers in the South. What I emotionally experienced during this past life session was that the slaves working in Annabelle's home had a great admiration and respect for her. They listened to her when she needed someone to talk to and they made sure she never felt lonely. By her choice to be "color blind," Annabelle felt affection and concern for these hard-working people that shared her life.

In my current life, it had also been my nature to accept all types of people, choosing to judge people not by the color of their skin but by how they behaved towards others. I cringed whenever I heard rude, thoughtless people spew racial slurs and I was overjoyed to witness the election of a black President in my lifetime.

Curiously, this session also gave me something else to think about. I told the professor that as a young girl I had an unusual fascination, almost an obsession, with two older black men. For years as I was growing up I was puzzled as to why I would have been so infatuated by them. I told the professor that after experiencing my life as Annabelle, the "why" had become somewhat clearer.

When I was six years old, my hard-working father was employed at a local bakery. The dishwasher he labored alongside of was a tall, lanky young black man named Albert. Being the type of man who loved all types of people, my good-natured father would on occasion invite Albert to drop by our house for a visit. I can distinctly recall that each time, I was utterly thrilled by his presence.

Even though Albert was a shy, quiet man and barely spoke more than two words to me, it didn't stop me from wanting to spend most of those visits sitting contently on his lap. I was always slightly mystified by my behavior, and sometimes I would think of Albert and wonder why had I had such a fond affection for this man I hardly knew?

When I was nine, my best friend Elizabeth and I decided to see a movie we had heard about at school. Since we were both attending Catholic school, the subject matter had piqued our interest. The movie was *Lilies of the Field*, starring Sidney Poitier. It was about a black American itinerant worker who encountered a group of East German nuns, who were convinced he has been sent to them by God to help build them a new chapel.

I remembered the first time I laid eyes on Sidney Poitier and how mesmerized I was. Tall, strong, and handsome, he portrayed Homer Smith, a man who was tough- minded and hard-working, yet there was also a kindness about him that made him lovable. Even at a young age, I felt his performance was outstanding and I was delighted later that year when he received an Academy Award for Best Actor. It was the first time a black man had ever won a competitive Oscar.

I left the movie that day in such high spirits that I happily sang the song "Amen" for weeks thereafter. From that day forward, I couldn't get enough of Mr. Poitier. I wanted to see every movie he starred in after that, such as *To Sir with Love* and *Guess Who's Coming to Dinner,* but I quickly learned my obsession would be limited by the amount of money my thrifty mother could spare. As I grew older my interest in these two men faded, but the question of why they had such an effect on me still lingered.

After I was done relaying my stories, it occurred to the professor and me that the reason that both Albert and Mr. Poitier had made such a significant impression on me as a young girl was that perhaps subconsciously they brought to mind Miles, who had once been my beloved servant.

As I got up from the comfortable recliner that had been my perch throughout the lengthy session, the professor gently reassured me that the next time we worked together the procedure would be much easier and that I should feel more willing and receptive to the whole process.

I left his office ecstatic about what I had just experienced. I couldn't wait to go home and tell anybody who would listen all about my three past lives. Their responses varied. A few found what I had to say fascinating. Most people thought it was weird. No matter, I wasn't expecting them to understand. It was something only I had experienced, so the negative views of others didn't keep me from freely expressing my thoughts and feelings about my regression

Early 1600s

Returning to the professor's office the following week, I was very enthusiastic to experience whatever mystical surprises this session had in store for me. Because I knew what to expect and was no longer fearful of the unknown, this time it was much easier for the professor to hypnotize me.

After giving me time to get comfortable and relaxed, the professor performed the same rather lengthy hypnosis routine as the last time. Once I was completely spellbound, he instructed me:

"Take a deep breath, let your thoughts settle somewhere, and let's see what happens."

Again I was guided to go through the long hallway that would lead me back in time. As I strolled past the many doors, I took my time in examining each one carefully. One particular door was tall and oddly narrow, its bottom half made from skillfully crafted wood, the top half of frosted glass. It felt strangely familiar to me. "When it feels right," the professor told me, "transition yourself through the door's opening and you'll find yourself standing in some unspecified place." Without hesitation, I eagerly grabbed the doorknob and opened it. "Where does it feel like you are?" I heard the professor ask. With his words still lingering, it didn't take long before a vivid image appeared in my mind.

I saw billowing, white rectangular sails, blowing in the wind, helping to glide a swift-moving vessel with a massive hull across a deep blue, white-capped sea that stretched endlessly for as far as the eye could see. Colorful flags, representing the standards of the monarchs of England, adorned its mighty masts.

As I observed this image, my first thought was that this was a pirate ship. That was the notion I had until the moment I saw myself standing on the bow of the deck. I knew then I couldn't be a pirate, because I was too well dressed. I was a tall man with a muscular build, dressed in black breeches, knee-high leather boots, and a red coat that appeared to be made of a much higher quality of material than the coats my shipmates wore. My black hat had a short crown with a wide brim, and I wore it confidently and slightly cocked to one side.

I was conversing with a small group of shipmates who were gathered around me. From our conversation it was clear that we were sailing in search of land. I also got the feeling that we were all extremely annoyed by the fact that we might be lost. We had been sailing on these uncharted seas for what seemed like an eternity, and to our dismay we had yet to encounter a single land sighting.

We were chosen for this expedition because of our curious and adventurous natures, and this trip was an undertaking we all had agreed to assume. We had all signed on fully aware that this exploratory mission would mean sailing for long periods of time. In the past, while sailing with a destination in mind, we knew what to expect as far as when we would arrive. This trip, however, was without destination.

My shipmates and I had had no idea how confined and frustrated we would all feel without knowing when, or even if, we would ever find what we had been looking for. Offering them words of encouragement to bolster their determination to succeed, I reminded them of the overwhelming satisfaction they would feel once we set foot upon a new land that they had discovered.

As my words began to resonate with the men, their renewed enthusiasm was displayed by three cheers and much back-slapping. Having already given this speech several times before on this journey, always getting the same results, I worried how much longer it would be before the men started showing signs of cabin fever and my reassuring words became meaningless.

During our long trip together, in order for us to keep our energy and enthusiasm up, we amused ourselves by challenging each other to sword fights, consuming a fair share of beer and wine, and retelling the same fabled stories we had heard a thousand times. I enjoyed the thrill and the sudden powerful onset of emotions sword fighting gave me. So far on our voyage I had been able to challenge every man at least twice a month, if not more.

Our long time together had afforded me the

ability to hone my craft and I had reached the point where I knew each opponent's signature moves and could anticipate their next actions even before they did. Although I was extremely proud at how skilled I had become, at times I had to play down those skills in order keep a competitive interest among the others.

I was known as a man who was quite clever and witty, and from the day we set sail, my shipmates relied upon me to keep their spirits high so that none of them ended up stark raving mad. When it came to making up imaginary stories, I was creatively talented. I was also quick to produce something humorous about our situation, or about someone's annoying habits. Add a little alcohol to the mix and the whole crew could entertain each other for hours.

As time passed, I found myself spending a great majority of my time down below in my cramped quarters. I recorded in my daily log book my personal thoughts about this bold undertaking we were on. Meticulously, I wrote about each lesson I had learned and the feelings I had felt, all the while hoping to share my insightful words with my family and friends back home in England one day.

Other times were spent lying on my bunk for hours at a time, thinking of nothing but how tired and impatient I was with the conditions we found ourselves in. There was nothing to focus on in that small, confined space but the steady ebb and flow of the water slowly moving the ship towards unfamiliar territory.

Being on that ship was nothing like being on today's cruise ships where you can easily entertain yourself by dropping by a casino or swimming in a fancy pool. I had to be creative in my thinking, constantly reinventing the day, or I could very possibly have lost my mind. One early morning, as I was dining below, my shipmates and I were suddenly taken aback by the shouts of elation coming from a deckhand situated high up in the crow's nest, proclaiming he had just spotted land. At first, we ignored what we were hearing. We had all seen the land mirage at some point in our long, tedious journey, usually following a night of excessive alcohol consumption, and each of us had cried wolf more than once.

But unlike those other times, the persistent deckhands continued shouting, begging us to come have a look. Their calls grew more convincing until they aroused our curiosity.

Reluctantly trudging our way up the stairs, our pace quickened as more men began to shout. As we advanced closer to the bow, we were stunned to find that this particular mirage was not fading. A silence fell over the ship as the realization of the moment began to sink in. After more than a year at sea, we had found what we had been looking for.

The closer we navigated the ship towards the magnificent vision stretched out before us, the more beautiful and real it became. Many of the crew, focused on the landscape emerging before us, hung perilously over the bow of the mighty ship as they tried to get a better view. We could now make out low-lying hills, lush with green vegetation and trees. The bluish-green water that hugged the shores of the endless white-and-pinkish sandy beaches was a sight we had never witnessed before.

We were all momentarily mesmerized by that truly wondrous sight, but then our dazed state turned into roars of laughter and hugs of joy that could not be contained. The cheering continued for the duration of our trip, until we finally felt the hard land below us slowing our ship. The men rushed to be the first one to plant their feet on solid ground, but it was I who was the fortunate one.

Once the shock of being on land began to subside, we made our way along the sandy shore, curious as to what we might find. As a few of my mates began examining those trees we had seen from the ship, we discovered they were coconut trees. The excitement started up again as one of the men scurried up a tree and proceeded to toss down its mouth-watering nut. Swords began flying as the men vigorously chopped away at the coconuts' hard shells. We wasted no time in devouring every last coconut on that tree.

After eating enough fish to drain the sea on our long journey, the refreshingly tasty coconuts we had just consumed were a welcome change in diet. We swore those coconuts were just about the best treat we had ever eaten. We spent the remainder of the day unloading our supplies from the ship's hold and setting up camp along the shore where we had first set foot. Later, as the glow from the sun set below the horizon, we celebrated our success long into the hours of darkness. We rejoiced in the fact that we had overcome a very difficult situation and had safely emerged triumphant.

The next day, as we searched the unfamiliar island for any signs of food or water, we stumbled across a small band of menacing-looking Indians. Their faces were covered with colorful masks, and each one held a long spear. We had wondered whether this island had inhabitants, but we certainly weren't expecting to run into any so soon. Judging by their startled reactions, it was obvious that they had not been expecting to encounter us either.

They stood defiant, but it was clear from their fidgety behavior that they were anxious and confused, and were not sure what to make of us. Because they were the ones holding those daunting- spears, coupled with the fact that we couldn't make out any facial expressions because of the masks, we all began offering them gifts of anything and everything we could to show them that we meant them no harm.

Through the wall of multi-colored faces, a very slight man began emerging to the front. The wall of men retreated and gave him room; however, they did not let down their guard. He was very short in stature, yet very much in command. He stood face-to-face with us and motioned for our leader to come forth. The men all turned and gave me the eye, and I stepped forward.

After completing what felt like an examination of my soul, the chief then turned his eyes to the ground before him and began assessing our gifts of goodwill. We hoped he would consider these gifts to be of a friendly nature, and not a gesture that would offend him.

A moment later, the chief spotted the hard, cream-colored handle of a hunting knife with a skillfully engraved leather sheath. Cautiously bending down to pick it up, he motioned to me that he would like to have it. I nodded in agreement. The chief then proceeded to remove one of his many necklaces and offered it to me. The necklace was made of tiny seashells held together by some sort of dried vegetation. I accepted his offering and smiled.

Without taking his eyes off of me, he removed his mask and revealed an ear-to-ear grin; at that instant each of the colored masks in the background was removed and tossed to the ground along with the spears. The chief motioned for his men to come forward and select the gifts they wanted; then each approached us to exchange something of theirs in return. By the time we were finished, a growing respect for one another had developed.

Motioning to us to follow them, the chief then led us deeper into the island's interior, to a clearing where the rest of his tribe lived. We arrived to find an array of huts made of various kinds of foliage, purposely positioned in a protective circle around the site. In the center was a common area where the women of the tribe were hard at work around a fire pit used for cooking and warmth. We also observed happy children playfully chasing each other. The children, in all their innocence, showed no fear of our presence and welcomed us with open arms. The hospitable chief let it be known that he wanted us to stay and share a meal with them, to which we gladly nodded our acceptance.

By now, we were all famished and eagerly looking forward to padding our hollow stomachs with a hot meal. That is, until we observed the women preparing what looked like a lifeless monkey. I jokingly uttered to the baffled men, "There's a first time for everything, mates. Like it or not, we should eat up and act like we love it, because there is no way we are going to offend them now."

At this point, the professor asked me if I could recall what my name was. I proudly mumbled something that sounded like, "John Powell." I remember thinking to myself that "John Powell" sounded like a good swashbuckler's name. I told the professor that soon we had grown to love that serenely beautiful island, and as a group we had unanimously decided that paradise was where we wanted to live and call home.

I began to tease the men and told them that this island wouldn't be much of a paradise for long if we didn't figure out how to bring some of our women from back home. As for alcohol, were going to need more of that too. It was agreed that a small group of us would remain behind on the island, while the others made the long trip back to England. Their mission was to return back to the island with enough willing people, a sufficient number of slaves, and an ample amount of supplies to start a colony, so that we could begin a new chapter to our life stories.

The peaceful serenity of the island had penetrated deep into my soul, and I no longer had a desire to return to the once-hectic, often-demanding life I had once lived. So I, along with a dozen like-minded men, chose to stay behind. The island's seductive vibrations had united us, and this was where I now belonged. With a heavy heart, I watched from the shore as the mighty ship set sail. As I bid farewell, I was painfully aware that it would be far into the future before I saw my comrades again.

Surprising not only myself, but also my mates on the island, I had decided to grow a beard. In the past I had always been remarkably well-groomed, but this new, rugged look suited my newfound life. My once-pristine uniform had been replaced with the basic clothing of a common deckhand, which was far more practical for me these days. Now that I was no longer required to fulfill an obligation, I was feeling as carefree as the refreshing southwest winds that blew in off the ocean.

My day usually started with me waking up far later than the rest of the island's inhabitants. No matter how hard I tried to get up with the sun, the years of continuously staying up late with the moon had become a ritual that I found impossible to break. During my long stretches spent traveling the open seas, I had watched my reliable timekeeper companion evolve from a tiny sliver to a bright, full moon. The information of time's passage he bestowed on me had led us to a respectful camaraderie. It would be thoughtless of me if I did not also mention my course-plotting friends the stars, and the stories they told through their constellations, which had helped to guide us on our many journeys. The night was a special time that I alone shared with the moon, and together we reminisced about old times past and new times to come.

Bright-eyed and ready to start my day, I

would wander over to the Indian village to check in with the people who had become my island family. I was immediately offered a bite to eat; later, with the help of a perfectly round coconut, I engaged in a quick game of kickball, which I had taught to the fun-loving children. Afterward I headed back to the beach, where the men of the tribe, enormously generous with their time and eager to share their ample skills and vast knowledge, were helping us build a small village of our own.

There was a united decision among the men to construct our huts along the picturesque beach. When we had first laid eyes on the mesmerizing shoreline, we spent a large amount of time staring at the beauty of the beach in disbelief. Maybe it was for sentimental reasons that we found ourselves drawn to build on the spot where we had first landed. Or maybe it was because we didn't want to miss out on the return of our seafaring friends.

The majority of each day was spent constructing our shelters, for the huts the Indians were helping us create took a very long time to perfect. Made from the bits and pieces of vegetation found throughout the island, the huts were tightly woven together. The small, one-room buildings were made to be strong and sturdy, with the ability to sustain many changes in weather.

Upon completion of our tiny village, we stood back and took a moment to admire our craftsmanship; we felt our pride swell from a sense of accomplishment. Now there was a secondary reason for building along the shore: we could hardly wait to show our fellow shipmates what we had been able to accomplish in their absence.

With the completion of our village I found myself, as in my days back on the ship, incredibly bored, with nothing to do. The majority of my time was now spent sitting on the beach, admiring the vast ocean and its splendor, while I patiently awaited the return of the long-absent ship. I daydreamed about the smooth taste of English ale and the soothing aroma from a finely made cigar, coupled with the laughter and stories we would undoubtedly be sharing with each other someday.

Many times during these daydreaming episodes I caught sight of a ship in the far- off distance, and with foolish impatience I jumped to my feet to get a better view. Sometimes, I would even swim out as far as my physical strength allowed me, to see if I could gain an even closer look. Relentlessly I was met with disappointment and a painful, longing feeling in my gut. It was that menacing mirage again, and the whirlwind of emotions that came with it. The elation was followed by the letdown, time and time again.

It was interesting to me that whether on land or at sea, the delirium brought on by an extreme desire for something was strangely similar. I pondered what caused my mind to allow this to happen and decided that once the supply ship had safely returned, the mischievous visions that had plagued me for years would disappear for good, and I would begin to feel whole again.

Almost two years had passed since the ship had set sail for England. As I made my nightly trip from my hut to the beach, my routine felt more like a rut these days. Nothing had changed in such a very long time. Each night as I sat on the beach outside my hut, my encounter with the moon was spent cursing at him, for now his only duty was to cruelly tell the passing of time. This moon was no longer my friend. He mocked me as, night after night, with his forever-changing shapes he would remind me of how long it had been since I had seen my friends.

As I doubted whether I would ever see my shipmates again, my mind began to wander and ruthlessly create a multitude of reasons as to why they had not yet returned. What if, once our comrades had returned home to their families, they changed their minds and decided not to return? Or perhaps somewhere along their journey they encountered stormy weather and turbulent seas that sank the ship? Losing hope with each day that passed, I knew that I needed to continue to remain strong and confident for the sake of the others still here on the island with me.

On one particular night, during one of my most relentless curses of a bright, full moon, I thought I saw the soft, steady glow of a lantern in the far-off distance. This time I chose to pay it no heed. I wasn't going to be fooled yet again. I had at long last learned my lesson on how deceptive the moon's light could be.

Soon I was lulled into a deep sleep by the repetitive sounds of the ocean as it gently lapped against the shoreline. After some time I was abruptly awakened by the sights and sounds of two of my mates screaming with gusto and jumping fully clothed into the waves. From behind me more men had begun streaming from their huts and wildly rushing into the water towards the optical illusion.

Once I emerged from my stupor, I also ran willingly towards the ocean and only when I was knee-deep in water did I realize that what I was experiencing was real. It was not my mirage but a ship, our mighty ship inching its way towards shore. "Hallelujah!" I shouted in relief. At long last, the day that I had feared would never come had finally arrived.

Finding it hard to control my emotions, I joined in with the others as they jumped up and down, splashing in the water and belting out loud yells of enthusiasm and joy. Aboard the ship, wildly waving hands only fueled my excitement to the point that I was afraid I might burst. It wasn't long before we were united with our long-awaited friends, and a whole new chapter in our lives was to begin.

Now lined up along the shore, we watched with great anticipation as the slow- moving vessel was eased into the shallow waters. A long wooden plank was lowered and our friends came pouring out, hooting and hollering, just as eager to see us as we were to see them. We rushed to embrace each other, and there was no shortage of smiles and laughter. Happiness overwhelmed me and for the first time in so very long, I felt complete.

My good friends brought with them from England a substantial amount of provisions including beer and wine, some musical instruments, a variety of seeds for planting, and enough building supplies to start our town. I was especially excited about the alcohol. It had been a long time since I had last enjoyed the strong, dark taste of an English brew.

Unloading the ship of its precious cargo took most of the day. A few men gathered enough wood to build a sizable fire on the beach just beyond our huts. As we worked together in blissful harmony, just as in times of old, we each speculated on what we would like our new life to be. Someone humbly suggested that one of the first things we should build was a chapel, so we could express our gratitude to God for our good fortune. Someone else insisted that we should immediately begin preparing the land for planting the seeds that would help provide an ample food supply.

Later that night, under the bright light of the full moon that I had now decided to pronounce blameless, we celebrated the day by getting bloody drunk and singing songs around a roaring fire that lasted into the wee hours of the morning.

It didn't take long before we decided to move from the beach and the huts we had outgrown, and build our town a little further inland. A splinter group was sent out in search of a location where the soil would be rich for planting, and where would be sheltered from any dangerous storms that should blow in off the ocean.

Gathering everyone close, I stated clearly that building a town would be quite an undertaking, requiring everyone's utmost cooperation, back-breaking labor, and long, tiresome hours. I informed them that just as the Indians had assisted us in building our huts, they had now graciously volunteered to help us achieve our dream. I wanted to have our town completed in record time so the people who had given up their lives back home to live here could have houses of their own and feel settled.

Weeks into the building, another ship arrived, bringing with it about sixty more settlers and a dozen or so slaves. That brought the total number of our colony to a little more than one hundred. Among these new arrivals was an attractive young lady who caught my roving eye. I noticed her silky blonde hair, which she wore tied back in a bun, and the graceful way she carried herself around the settlement. She had been hand-picked by the others to prepare the food eaten on the tediously long voyage to the island, for she had an exceptional ability to whip up delicious meals out of practically nothing. That beautiful young lady now spent her time and talents preparing meals for us.

One night, after revealing my thoughts to the moon about my recent good fortune, I was meandering back from the beach when I stumbled upon her, sitting in her hut with her back toward the window. To my surprise, her lush mane of light-colored hair was let down and she was brushing it. I stopped and stared as she patiently and meticulously brushed the long locks that glistened in the candlelight with every brushstroke.

Sensing my presence, she pivoted to face the window and spotted me. Embarrassed by having been exposed, I wanted to duck or turn and flee, but my betraying feet failed me and I could not move. Frozen where I stood, I could feel my face blush hot shades of dark red as beads of moisture began to surface on my brow. Thankfully, the darkness of the night shielded my awkward condition from her observant eyes.

Rising from her chair, she gently glided towards the open window. As she slowly lowered the cloth to cover the window, she flashed a smile and her pleasant expression sent a sensation pulsating through my entire body like nothing I had ever felt before. Once she was out of sight, I was able to regain my composure and continue on my way. Unable to contain the enamored expression rapidly forming on my face, I carried a whimsical smile with me all the way back to my hut. As I lay on my bed, the memory of our brief encounter and her gentle, heartwarming appearance lingered in my mind until I had fallen fast asleep.

At this point in the session, I relayed to the professor that I got the feeling I was going to marry the girl and that our baby would be the first one born to any of us on the island.

Ever since the night when the enticing young woman had caught me staring at her in the window, the two of us had been inseparable. Before long she spent her nights cozily sitting beside me on the sandy beach, under the light of the moon, as I regaled her with stories of the adventurous life I had once lived.

Months later I married the pretty girl I had grown to love so dearly, in the small church that we had built on the edge of town. We finished building our home shortly after we wed and just in time for the birth of our first baby, a healthy rosy-cheeked boy. We named him James after King James I of England who had, on the year we first landed on the island, suffered a stroke and died shortly thereafter.

Years ago, when I had been an ambitious young sailor, this was a life I would never have imagined possible. Our baby was a precious gift from God, and along with my wife they both brought me so much happiness. To think that she and I had created such a beautiful child filled me with a sense of pride.

I was once known as a free-spirited man who would pick up and travel on a moment's notice. Now I was a man who could not dream of being away from his family for more than a minute, something that anyone who had known me would have never expected. I was very proud of all I had accomplished, and I would not have exchanged this life for all the gold in the world. Had I not been courageous enough to leave England and travel in uncharted waters for what had seemed like an eternity, I would never have discovered this beautiful island that we now called home, and none of the happiness I now possessed would have ever been.

The professor asked me what I called this new land. I answered, "Barbados." He then asked me to move forward in time to the event of my death.

During the many years that had passed, the dreams and desires we had for our town were completed and my devoted wife had given birth to four more children. However, the cruel passing of time and a physically demanding life had taken an immense toll on me. I now inhabited a shrunken, worthless body that no longer cooperated with me as it had so faithfully done for many years. Once a tall, strong man who could do the work of ten men, I was now unable to do the work of even one. Barely getting around anymore, I knew that my time to depart this life was rapidly approaching. My body tried to fight it, my mind tried to wish it away, but I knew this was one struggle I was going to lose.

As of late, I had been spending most of my

time in bed. My attentive wife, knowing that I would most likely attempt to do something that was beyond my means, had devoted her every waking hour to be by my side. Putting my wants and wishes before her own, she faithfully tended to all my needs. I appreciated the love, but I wished that I hadn't needed the help. In lucid moments, I found myself torn between thanking God for the good life I had lived and begging Him for one more chance to repeat this life again.

Sleep consumed me on a daily basis and my wife woke me only to give me nourishment and water. One day I dreamt that loved ones who had died before me were calling me to join them. Awaking briefly, my eyes searched the room. The warm light and slight breeze from the open window drew my attention towards it. Viewing the sight beyond the window, I beamed with pride at the town that I so painstakingly helped build. My sadly smiling wife, sitting in a chair beside my bed, gently stroked my hair as if to say she understood that it was my time to go, and I gently gave in.

Closing my eyes for the last time, at the age of eighty-six, I passed from that life surrounded by the love of my devoted family. Bathed in a calming white light that peacefully enveloped my soul, I felt myself begin to rise. I hovered, without discomfort, over my barely recognizable body and I could see my children and grandchildren gathered around my bed. Cherishing that life and everything it had to offer, I found it hard to leave. Wishing to console all who had loved me, I willfully lingered for as long as I could. Then, unexpectedly, a gentle sensation urging me to move on radiated through me just as the poignant scene below me began to fade.

I now found myself floating freely in complete and uncontrollable happiness, when out of nowhere some warm, friendly-looking people came into being. Greeting me with outstretched arms, one by one they approached and affectionately embraced me. I didn't know any of these accommodating souls, but they made me feel welcome.

After my brief encounter with the unfamiliar faces, I did not go to the picturesque garden I had visited before, but instead found myself surrounded by pure whiteness, like that of freshly fallen snow. Immeasurable time had elapsed and I was confused. I wondered why I was being secluded in some kind of way station. What was my purpose for being here? Was I waiting for someone, or was I waiting for something to happen? Strangely, this long period of waiting felt very much like the life I had just left behind.

The professor asked me to move on from that life and return to the hallway with its many doors. He again instructed me to walk to the door that beckoned me. Doing as I was told, I walked the hallway until a distinctive red door with a unique brass knob caught my eye, and that was the one I chose.

On the other side I found a blinding brightness that all but disappeared upon my entering. Off in the distance, a picture was slowly beginning to form. As I approached to gain a better look, I could see the figure of a woman and the shape of a horse, and at that moment it became clear I was about to enter my next life.

The Champion

Immediately I sensed that the stylish and athletic young woman standing at the entrance of a spacious outdoor arena was me. I was fashionably dressed so that I stood out, and my prized horse stood tall and statuesque beside me. I could now hear the sound of people conversing in the grandstands; the sound echoed throughout the arena while the sight of many horses preparing to compete got my adrenaline going.

For months my remarkable horse and I had been mentally and physically training to perform in this show jumping competition, the largest, most important show of the year. To be here in my hometown arena that was filled with avid, horse-loving people, all emitting high amounts of energy and enthusiasm, was what my horse and I lived for.

Immersed in the mounting excitement, my eyes scanned the massive grandstand, catching sight of several socially prominent women dressed to impress.

The professor interjected: "What year is it?"

"I don't know," I answered. "Maybe early 1900s." I described women in Edwardian-style clothing, twirling their fancy parasols as they mingled with others, but it was hard for me to say. I told him that this once-a-year spectacular event brought out the fashionably elite in droves. It was the most popular place to be at this time of year, and everyone who was anyone could be found here.

For my horse and myself, performing before

large crowds of spectators was a special time shared between us. I was in high spirits to be there with my best friend. Through long hours of hard work we had built up quite a sterling reputation as the team that couldn't be beat, and many show jumpers envied our success. We shared a tremendous amount of trust and profound respect for one another, and together we had grown to have a great understanding and appreciation for all the show jumping events we had participated in. Because of our high aspirations we had, over the years, won numerous trophies and blue ribbons. Over the span of our career, I had put together quite a collection of scrapbooks containing our blue ribbons as well as newspaper clippings that people had written about our success. Winning so many competitions allowed the two of us a very comfortable lifestyle.

I expected we would easily win the most coveted trophy during this year's competition, too. More importantly, the real prize was the great pleasure we received from performing together. My horse was my family and we had grown inseparable over the years. I told the professor that, at this point in my life, my horse might be my only family. I searched my mind for some memory of a family, but I had no recall. Either they had passed on, or they just were not that important to me.

I told the professor that my name was Beth, short for Elizabeth, and that my last name was Morgan. I described to him how I sat sidesaddle on my horse and that I looked to be wearing the latest in fashion. I was fabulously dressed in a teal-green, long-sleeved jacket adorned with six silver buttons, three on each side. Connected to the buttons were three decorative silver chains that draped across my chest. I complemented the jacket with a matching teal split skirt and a pair of white bloomers tied at the knee. To complete my look, I wore my finest leather riding boots and a black flat-top derby with a matching long teal-green scarf tied around the brim so that it draped down the middle of my back. My horse and I were admired just as much for our polished looks as we were for our exceptional talent, and looking our best at every competition always left a good impression.

My horse was himself exceedingly handsome. His big, brown eyes had a way of beguiling me and touching me to my core. He complemented me well with his soft, shiny, reddish-brown coat, and a dark-brown, almost black, mane and tail. What really made him stand out from all others was a white, star-shaped patch on his nose. This served to announce that his fame was meant to be.

The professor asked me to go back as far as I could in this life and tell him how I got to be where I was.

I revealed that at a young age, I was permitted by the arena workers to spend my spare time there unaided, and that was when my love for

136

horses began. Sitting on the hard wooden bleachers inside the covered red-and-white-painted grandstand, I watched in wonder as the passionate riders and their practiced horses would compete and achieve victory. From a hunger building deep within my soul, I realized that when I grew older this was the kind of fame I wanted to achieve.

One day I met an outgoing older gentleman named Gus who boarded several horses at the stable. I found him to be a very likeable man and the more time we spent getting to know each other, the more comfortable I felt in his presence. In time I revealed to him the passionate dreams I had for a successful future in show jumping. Gus, being mighty impressed with my high-spiritedness, invited me to assist him on weekends with the daily routine of tending to his horses. Working intently by his side, I clung to his every word as he shared his vast knowledge of horses and show jumping with me. Day after day, he patiently listened as I shared with him my desire to be the best show jumper ever. Over time, "Old Gus" (as he liked to be called) and I developed a special friendship. He was the family I was missing and needed, and I believed he felt the same way about me.

In my early teens, Old Gus taught me to ride sidesaddle and jump fences using one of his own horses. His attentiveness and his belief in me were like a dream come true. Every day, hours were devoted to my training and soon I was presentable enough to enter into local competitions. After I won several trophies, I overheard Old Gus bragging to everyone at the stable about how proud he was of me, which only fueled my desire for more success.

Shortly after I placed first in a major show jumping competition, Old Gus surprised me by rewarding me with a horse of my own. He was a young thoroughbred, and top of the line among the other boarded horses. Batting his long, thick lashes and gently nudging me with his nose, "Danny Boy" flirted his way into my heart, and it was love at first sight. From that day, I was totally devoted to him and he wanted nothing more than to please me. Danny was clever and keen, and he instinctively understood every task that I asked him to perform. Together we made a wonderful, unstoppable team that had brought us to where we were today.

The start of the show was just minutes away, and just as the patrons showed off their finest by strutting around the grandstand, Danny and I also paraded around the showground right before it was our turn to compete. From the minute we stepped out onto the field, the crowd erupted into roars and loud applause. The elation and pride I felt within me shone through my smile. Proudly, Danny and I walked side-by-side with our heads held high. I waved and blew kisses to the welcoming crowd until we had walked around the entire arena. The applause slowly subsided as we prepared to begin.

As I mounted my horse, I could feel my pulse racing. From high on my perch I assessed the multicolored and creatively designed course. Gently leaning over, I whispered kindhearted words of encouragement into Danny's perked-up ears. He signaled to me with a nod of his head that he understood that it was time for us to do what we did best: perform. After a brief pause, the whistle blew and we were off and running. As I focused on the task at hand, the crowded grandstand completely disappeared and only Danny and I existed. As we took flight over our first two-bar jump, I felt united with my horse.

Our first jump was perfection. We were well on our way to our next trophy; I could feel it. As we approached the next hurdle, a three-bar jump, his muscular body glided gracefully over the obstacle and cleared it with ease. Then came a fairly challenging jump with a greater degree of technical difficulty, but we were trained and ready. I was confident this jump would be no different than the rest.

Effortlessly we cleared the white picket fence and the shallow pond of water on the other side, but as we landed Danny's leg crumbled beneath him as if it was a pillar of sand. In a split second we both plunged head first onto the hard ground below. I was stunned to find myself curled up in a ball on the field, moaning in pain and no longer up on my horse. Dazed and confused by the initial shock of what had just happened, it took me a moment before I realized that Danny's leg had shattered.

Desperately I made my way towards his injured body writhing in the dirt. Watching Danny in pain superseded any physical pain that I might have felt from our tumble to the ground. Catching sight of me, my loyal horse bravely struggled to stand and greet me. I cried out to Danny to stay down, but it was too late. I tearfully watched as, unable to regain his footing, he painfully collapsed back onto the ground. Standing over my poor horse, seeing him in such agonizing pain, I felt a huge ache in my chest, as if someone was reaching in and pulling out my heart.

Sensing that what I was about to tell the professor would be unpleasant, I forced myself to continue. The compassionate show officials only confirmed what I already felt deep within my aching heart. Danny's injuries were too severe, and there was nothing they could do to save him. Sympathetically they explained that the right thing, the most humane thing they could do for him right now, would be to shoot him and put him out of his misery. I was in shock and completely numb as I listened to their words. The next words out of my mouth were a heart-wrenching, "Oh God, no! This just can't be happening, not my horse, not my beloved Danny. You all don't understand, he's a champion." The sound of the gun's discharge was followed by an eerie silence. There on the ground before me, my beautiful horse lay motionless. In one split second, life had abandoned his body and I was left standing there, emotionally devastated.

I revealed to the professor that all the life-changing emotions I experienced with Danny's death were the same feelings of anguish and disbelief I had lived through in my present life when I first heard that my husband had died in a car accident. Just like Steve, Danny had been my world and now my world was heartbreakingly empty.

"How could we not have made that jump?" I thought to myself. After our many years of endless practice and prize-winning competitions, it was incomprehensible that this could have happened to Danny and me. Many questions of "why?" kept playing over and over again in my mind until I collapsed in uncontrollable sobs next to his lifeless body. "Oh, my poor Danny. My heart is so broken and I ache for you. How am I ever going to go on living without you, my beloved best friend?"

The considerate professor decided it was now time for me to move away from this emotional scene and forward to my next memory.

After Danny's death, my good friends and fellow competitors tried in vain to persuade me to return to the arena and take up again where I had left off. These caring sympathizers were extremely supportive and spent many hours consoling me in my heartache and confusion. A gracious friend of mine offered to give me one of her prize show horses in an effort to get me show jumping again, but even that kind gesture was unsuccessful.

Eventually I gave in to their relentless urging and for a brief time I dispassionately started training again. I even competed in a few events, but it was pointless. I no longer had the excitement or desire. My driving passion to participate had died along with my best friend. Nothing was ever going to come close to replacing the spiritual bond

I'd had with my devoted Danny. I simply didn't care any more.

I choose instead to retire altogether from competing, and I obtained a job tending to the horses at the arena stables, the same job "Old Gus" had done so many years ago. Devoting my time to the well-being of the horses was what would be best for me now. Mentally and physically connecting with the horses would give my soul great comfort, and I hoped that over time it would heal my shattered spirit.

Now my long, solitary days consisted of getting up at the break of dawn and making my way down to the stables to ensure that all the horses were well fed. When that chore was done, I saw to it that each horse got some form of physical exercise. Most days this consisted of inspiring them to run several laps around the large wooden corral that was adjacent to the barn. When all of those chores were completed, it was on to their favorite part of the day, when I performed the role of the conscientious brusher of their beautiful coats.

As I headed towards them carrying my little blue bucket filled with assorted brushes, often the more outgoing horses would shake their heads up and down, neighing loudly with excitement. When the happy horses made this friendly, "we're glad to see you" gesture, it always put an ear-to-ear grin on my face, knowing that I was about to engage in a task that they loved. Of course there were always a few temperamental ones that would pull back their ears to signal that I was not to bother them today.

The lengthy brushing of their coats was not an easy task, especially when you had several horses all fancying their own special beauty treatment. With short firm strokes, I would move my arm in a circular motion to loosen the dead hair, hay, or burrs that might be causing them the slightest irritation. Brushing them daily not only kept their coats smooth and shiny, but it was also necessary to help keep bacteria away from their skin. It took a good deal of elbow grease and a clear knowledge of which brushes were used for the manes and tails and which were used for their coats.

As I labored away on my act of love, I remembered something Old Gus once told me long ago: that the outside of a horse does well for the inside of a man. He was a wise man who knew that the act of brushing was therapeutic; it relieved stress and it also gave you time to think. Once I had completed my mission of good hygiene, the grateful horses expressed to me their gratitude by gently resting their sweet-smelling heads on my shoulder or by softly rubbing their smooth muzzles against my body. It was their special way of telling me that they were thankful for my undivided attention, and those loving acts alone made all my hard work worthwhile.

Shortly after Danny's dreadful death, I sold the country estate that had been my home for many years. The precious memories of the life Danny and I had once shared there preoccupied my every thought, causing me to lack energy and the ability to think clearly. Living there was just too painful, and for my own sanity I needed to become someone different. Once my decision to move and start anew was made, my close friends and fellow equestrians abandoned all hope of me ever returning to my previous competitive lifestyle. As time went on I saw less and less of them.

I now lived a quiet life in a modest little cottage, located on the same property as the arena for it was an easy walk from there to the stables. The light-blue cottage with its large front porch was encircled by a short, white picket fence. Inside the fence and off to one side, I had planted a simple yet beautifully pleasing rose garden that had turned into a bit of an uplifting hobby when I was not working at the stables.

The inside of my home was modest and lacking in décor. I had sold most of my stylish and expensive possessions prior to moving there. The main things I brought with me were my favorite, well-crafted wooden rocking chair, my stylishly designed four- poster bed, and a common kitchen table with chairs, but not much else. My decorations consisted mostly of my trophies placed around the bedroom and adorning the mantle of my fireplace. The house was orderly and clean in appearance, and that was probably because I was not there that often.

I had also sold all the pretty dresses I'd worn for competitions and for the socializing my success had demanded. Over time I had transformed from an elegant, well-known, well-dressed young lady into a withdrawn, dressed-down tomboy working at the horse stables. My wardrobe now consisted of baggy men's pants with suspenders, flannel shirts, leather boots, and a big, floppy hat. At the arena, where I was once acknowledged as the star, I now heard whispers from people who stared. They thought I didn't know what they were saying. They assumed I was oblivious to the fact that I was gossiped about as the mysteriously reclusive horse lady.

Living alone had its disadvantages. There were days when, sitting at my kitchen table, I found myself feeling incredibly lonely. And then, one day while I was out shopping at the local open-air market, I stumbled upon a man selling a friendly young dog he had found abandoned. Saddened by the discarded dog's troubles and feeling a sense of a kinship between the two of us, I bought the dog. I named him Ruff for the funny sound of his bark. His short, barrel-shaped body was covered with a bluish-gray coat, and his eyes, one brown and one blue, made him unique. He looked like one of those sheepherding dogs.

It didn't take long for this lively ball of fur to make himself right at home. Soon our morning trip down to the stables was the highlight of Ruff's day, and I do believe the horses were just as thrilled to see him as they were to see me. In the corral, during the daily workout Ruff liked to pretend that he was skillfully herding the horses as he vigorously chased behind them. After a hard day's work Ruff, who loved the fresh, cool evening breezes, preferred spending his nights out on the front porch, guarding the house, just in case he would have to protect me from some furry critter that wandered near.

Sometimes, in the summertime when it was unbelievably hot and humid, Ruff and I would stroll down to the big horse barn at nightfall. Finding ourselves an acceptable pile of hay to curl up on, we would fall asleep to the soothing sounds of the many horses breathing nearby.

The professor asked me to recall the next memory in this life.

I was in my early sixties now and sadly, I

was no longer working at the stables that much anymore. A painful case of arthritis had afflicted certain parts of my body, such as my knees, shoulders, and lower back. My physical condition had deteriorated to the point where it was hard for me to get around without the help of a sturdy cane. Even the simple act of climbing up and down the stairs at my own house had become too difficult to bear. On good days, I was fortunate in that I could still manage to slowly shuffle my way out to the garden to care for my precious roses. More often, my time was idly spent out on the front porch in my old rocking chair. Lying on his blanket beside me was my old, faithful companion Ruff, who now had a bit of arthritis himself, and I gently stroked his soft fur.

Some days, when the wind was blowing just right, I could hear the enthusiastic attendees clapping and cheering at a show jumping competition. Those sounds would transport me back to when my beloved horse Danny and I were the stars of the show and our admirers were expressing their excitement for us. Those thoughts of Danny could easily bring a smile to my lips as I recaptured memories of my beautiful horse and the enjoyable experiences we had shared. And in a split second, if I let my thoughts go there, I could summon up the heartbreak of our last day together and it could quickly bring tears to my eyes. Lingering, heartfelt memories of my competitive days were still bittersweet, even though it seemed so long ago.

The professor asked to move forward to the time of my death.

At age eighty-six, it was clear the end of my life was near. Looking back over the years gone by, I had fully accepted the life I had lived and the choices I had made, and I was going to leave this life having no regrets.

I was living alone. My faithful companion Ruff had passed away quite some time ago, and the big porch seemed so empty without him. His food and water bowl were still positioned by the front door, with his tattered bed nearby. I did not have the heart to remove them.

My arthritis had now spread to every inch of my body and these days I could barely manage to care for myself, let alone my cherished roses. The garden itself wasn't as perfectly manicured as it once has been, but my roses remained just as beautiful. Each and every one of my vibrantly blooming varieties still filled me with pride and brought me great joy.

Early on a spring morning, I fancied that a vase of freshly cut roses would be just what my kitchen table needed. Sensing that a cool breeze was in the air, I gently wrapped myself in an old knitted shawl before stepping out onto the porch. After painfully descending the stairs, with a cane in my hand I slowly inched my way toward the rose garden. As I paused to take a moment to admire my roses and all their beauty, my heart ceased to beat within my chest. As I struggled to gasp my last breath, my lifeless body simultaneously slumped to the ground and my life as I had known it came to an end.

I didn't linger much after I died, not like my reluctant departure from my previous life. This time I was whisked away quickly, zooming higher and higher until I had this incredible urge to scream, "Wheeeeeee!!!!!" at the top of my lungs like a young child on a rollercoaster ride.

Yet again, I found myself in that same fantasy-like garden, the one with the crystal-clear steam that seemed to endlessly wind its way past perfectly manicured flowerbeds. Echoes of children's laughter filled the air, interrupting the dream-like state that momentarily possessed me. As I scanned the garden to find the source of the laughter, my eyes caught sight of a bright glow and a large, dark, shadowy figure inside. As the bright light surrounding the silhouette faded, I could hardly believe my eyes. It was Danny, my beloved horse, grazing in a field of tall grass.

I quickly and passionately ran towards him as love once again filled my heart. Spotting me out of the corner of his eye, he was unable to contain his excitement and suddenly belted out a welcoming neigh. My kisses covered his velvet nose, as I gently cradled his big, sweet-smelling head in my hands. As I wrapped my loving arms around his soft, smooth neck I snuggled my face up against his and showed him the same love and affection I had done so long ago.

As the memories flooded in, my eyes overflowed with tears. Feelings of pure joy overwhelmed me. For so long, every prayer I had ever prayed, every dream I had ever dreamt, was to once again gaze into Danny's big, brown eyes and feel his warm breath against my cheek. Being here in this amazing place, caressing the neck of my precious Danny, was truly a dream come true.

Reluctantly my attention was diverted away from my horse by the silhouettes of many people, off in the far distance, all doing their own thing. I sensed their glances, but for some strange reason they were not at all interested in approaching me. It almost felt as if Danny and I were back at the arena and those people were watching us from the grandstands.

The professor interjected, "Would you like them to talk to you?"

"No," I replied. "Much of my life was like that, people off in the distance living their own lives. They don't really interest me."

"Is there a place you stay there? Can you go anywhere?"

"No, the people I see are on the outside of where I am with Danny. It's like we're in a bubble."

Glancing around at my surroundings, I was curious about the place I found myself in. I pondered that what I was experiencing was very much like my life on earth. The distance I felt right then from the shadowy figures was just like the same emotional aloofness I had felt in my human relationships. And now, for some reason, I had been brought back to this place to be reunited with the only thing that ever mattered to me in that life: my beloved horse. As I peacefully led Danny down a path toward the main garden, whispers from an inner voice revealed the answer to me. I understood that as a result of my caring love for animals and the decent and honest life I had lived, my reward was to come here, reunite with my horse, and feel love again.

And what a reward it was. My whole existence now consisted of the forever happiness of loving my horse and the contentment I felt while riding Danny around this magical garden. I was happy. That is, until after what seemed like endless time had elapsed and the importance of my horse, that once had meant so much to me, eventually began to fade away.

Growing extremely restless because my freedom here was limited to the garden, feelings of being "stuck" began to overwhelm me. For some reason, I remained here much longer than I had the other times I had visited this place. Previously, upon arriving, I was promptly assigned a new life. This time, to my dismay I found myself in a situation where I hadn't any place to go. I had incredibly strong urges to move on, but when and to what?

I had been absent from human existence for such a vast amount of time that when the time finally arrived for me to move on, I welcomed it with an overwhelming eagerness. Feeling the core of my essence floating away at a snail's pace was indeed a stark contrast from my rollercoaster arrival. Ready and eager to embark on a new, exciting experience, I willingly drifted into my new life.

Prehistoric Times

I was surprised and somewhat perplexed to find myself being born in a shelter of hollowed-out rock, nestled high atop a snow-covered mountain. The shallow cavity was dark and damp, except for the glow and warmth of a brightly burning fire located at the entrance to the cave. I was born a male in this life. My mother, after silently grimacing in pain, snatched me up in her arms and quickly wrapped me tight in warm fur skins to shield me from the bitter cold.

Snuggled warmly within my mother's secure embrace, my blurry eyes strained to focus on her welcoming smile above. With my mother's gentle cradling, my restlessness and uncertainty of what lay ahead vanished. My anxious thoughts had been replaced by feelings of contentment and love.

In my next memory of this life I found myself to be a young man, about the age of seventeen, with long, stringy, brown hair that extended past my shoulders. I had thick, bushy eyebrows and a broad nose. I was tall and robust, and did not possess the stooped-over posture one would expect a caveman to have. My physical features looked to be more like that of a Cro-Magnon man, and not the ape-like appearance of a Neanderthal. We did not speak, but communicated through gestures and crude grunting noises.

I wore clothes made of thick, warm animal fur and my feet were covered with animal hides tied together by thin strips of leather. My mother had been able to stitch together the clothing we wore by using sharp bone needles that my father had skillfully carved for her. I also wore an animal tooth necklace that was a proud trophy from a prized kill.

I was still living in the same cave where I had been born. My mother and father lived there, as did my younger brother and my grandmother. My mother's brother, who had died from a severe injury during a hunt, and my grandfather, who had died from old age, had lived with us while I was growing up. When I was younger, I also had a baby sister, but she died not long after being born.

From a very early age, I was taught that in order for our clan to survive I must become a skilled hunter of the many thunderous herds that stopped to graze in the valleys below. One of the many things my wise grandfather taught me was his discovery that by using certain rocks he could draw pictures of color. On the walls inside our cave, he cleverly created rough drawings depicting the different animals he had killed when he had first learned to hunt. His jagged sketches told the story of how he tracked his prey and then killed it with his powerful spear. Then he taught me to hunt, and through his encouraging ways I learned to be just as cunning and as brave a hunter as he.

As I grew taller and stronger, I provided for our family's survival by putting into effect all that I had learned. My first kill was that of a stocky, muscular wolverine. He might not have been very big, maybe thirty pounds or so, but he was mean and nasty, with a pungent odor that stayed with me for days. My dark-furred opponent put up a vicious fight, but in the end I was the victor.

Some years later, when my brother and I had become practiced hunters, it was decided that my grandfather, who was now too old to hunt, would be left behind at the cave. Slow and weak, he had become a hindrance and it was now far too dangerous for him to track down prey. No longer of any use, this proud man, once a tower of strength, lost his will to live and departed from life not long after that fateful decision.

It was our father who taught us the artful technique of crafting the spearheads we used for hunting. He began by directing my brother and me to gather up flint rocks. Next, he had us collect wooden sticks that we had already shaped into handles, and the strips of leather needed to complete our task. With stone hammers we painstakingly chipped away layers of hard, grayish-black rock, giving it a rough, blade-like appearance. Then with wood or bone tools we would carve out small flakes that would refine a blade's edges and tip, until it was sharp enough to penetrate an animal's hide.

To attach the stone to the spear handle, we created flanges on the base of the spearhead. We then readied the wooden handles by soaking them in water to soften. A slit was then cut vertically into one end of the handle to provide a place for the spearhead to fit. It was then fixed to the shaft with strong straps of leather.

Besides a constant fire, these spears were our primary means of survival. We used them for protection from the mighty cave bear and for hunting prey like the large arctic reindeer. But mostly what we hunted was that prized prey, the strong and powerful woolly mammoth. Standing nearly ten feet tall and covered in a thick layer of shaggy hair, the mammoths' high, rounded heads appeared knob-like, and on their backs they had a large shoulder hump. Mammoths were dangerous because of their enormous size, but they were also slow-moving and easy to pursue.

When I was young, the purpose of the mammoth's distinctly curved tusks, which could grow as long as sixteen feet, escaped me. I knew they used them as weapons to ward off vicious attacks, but I thought they must serve another purpose as well. One day, while out scouting prey with my grandfather, I witnessed these beasts foraging in the valley by using their tusks as shovels to clear the deep snow from the ground and reach the seed pods buried below. I wondered no more.

Our close-knit family preferred to live a solitary lifestyle, but during scarce times we would join other clans living on the nearby mountains to track this large, often dangerous prey. Hunting in larger numbers almost always lessened the chance of anyone getting seriously hurt, and the more trackers we had, the better our chances were for a more successful pursuit. When provoked, the assertive creatures we hunted could get extremely aggressive. Without a moment's notice, they could easily kill, as they did my uncle. To protect ourselves, we sought out the smallest, weakest, or oldest males of the herd and made them our primary target.

Our line of attack was to distract a mammoth's attention by using some of us as bait, and then the strongest and bravest hunter would step forward. He would stand a safe distance from but directly in front of the intimidating creature, and his loud shouts and frantically waving arms would befuddle the unsuspecting beast. While the fearless distracter commanded the mammoth's attention, another daring and bold hunter would grab onto the beast's solid, hairy body and dangle perilously off his hindquarters. Now with the creature totally distracted and thrown off balance, the rest of us would approach quietly from behind and stab him with our many spears. We had to be quick, get dangerously close, and stab the hostile bull repeatedly with great physical force. Mammoths, because of their massive size, do not succumb easily to their injuries.

This exhausting process would take up most of the day, but the mammoths' hairy skin provided us with warm clothes and thick blankets. Their tusks were crushed into a fine dust and used to make medicine. And their deep layers of meat and blubbery fat supplied enough food to help sustain us through the long, snowy winter months.

One particular winter was long and harsh. Each year the already cruel winters had grown increasingly more intolerable. My father told me that this winter had been the worst cold season he had ever experienced. Numb from the frigid coldness that penetrated deep into my bones, the only thing that I could still feel was an overwhelming sense of hunger.

Our mammoth kill should have provided a more-than-ample food supply to carry us through, but this was no ordinary winter. Our fixed rations had dwindled down to only a few scraps a day for each of us. And to make matters worse, the heartless, blinding snow outside our cave was taunting us, daring us to venture out into its darkness. It had become imperative to our survival that we brave the outside elements soon in an urgent and frantic search for more food.

My father, growing increasingly worried about the fate of his family, discussed leaving the cave with my brother in search of rabbit, white foxes, or anything that would help us to survive. Wrapping themselves completely in several layers of animal hides to protect their weakened bodies from the biting cold, they bravely stepped out into the relentless storm. But the weather proved too severe and forced them to retreat empty-handed back to the cave.

Because of that failed attempt, my father found it necessary to face the only option he had left: banishing my grandmother (his own mother) out into the blizzard to die. I watched unflinchingly as my father coldly motioned for her to leave the warmth of the cave. Bravely she rose, and went willingly. She had lived long enough to know that it was a sacrifice she had to make for her family to survive. There was an eerie silence as I watch her solemnly leave her home for the last time, and in that moment I was suddenly reminded of my younger sister who, years ago, also had to be sacrificed in a similar manner.

When my little sister was born, she was very small and frail. It was obvious to all that she would not be able to endure this tough environment. With no goodbyes and no emotions, my father took my baby sister from my mother's arms and she was placed out in the snow to die. After their sacrifices, my grandmother and sister were never spoken of again.

Now, with only a few days of food left and my family feeling beyond hopeless, that night we woke to find that the prevailing winds and strong snowfall had subsided long enough for my father and brother to exit the cave. After a brief absence they both returned, having had no trouble finding us food. Animals that were as hungry as we were had also been held captive by the snow, and were out taking advantage of the break in the hostile weather. My mother and I were elated to know that soon the severe hunger pains that had been plaguing us would all but disappear.

A few months later, the harsh conditions of that recent winter had passed. The view outside the cave was beginning to show signs of a long-awaited springtime. My aging father was frustrated with the ominous winter season, and after that terrible winter he decided to move us to a different location, lower down the mountain. This would ensure that the weather would be less brutal and the snowfall less deep, but it did pose some risk. Undoubtedly we would encounter more predatory animals and expose ourselves to a different kind of danger. Now that my brother and I had grown to be strong young men able to defend ourselves, my father was willing to take that chance.

My father told us to start gathering up our things. We immediately created a stretcher-like device that would enable us to easily carry our belongings. My brother and I had already been taught how to construct one by taking two long sticks, placing them parallel to each other and securely attaching a stretched piece of animal hide across the middle with strong strips of leather. After we had piled on it all of our miscellaneous items from inside the cave, the four of us took one last look around to make sure we hadn't left anything behind.

Certain that we had done everything that needed to be done, my father motioned to us that he was now ready to embark on our search for a different cave. My brother and I, being the strongest, grabbed the ends of the long sticks and proceeded to lift our heavy load. After taking a few steps, I paused briefly to take one last glance back at the cave that had been my home for so long. I had sadness in my heart as I embraced the memories of what had been and would never be again, and of the loved ones who had been lost to us forever. Though deep in thought, I remembered that there was no time for weakness and that I must move on. With our lean bodies in motion, we carried our belongings and my father and mother led the way as we advanced down the mountainside in search of a new home.

After traveling a great distance down the steep mountain, my father understood that my brother and I had grown weary from carrying our heavy load and found us shelter among some large boulders we had stumbled upon. It was to be nightfall soon, so we would settle for the night. To ensure that we were kept warm and safe, we first found dry wood for a fire. We then foraged for something to eat.

My father decided that it would be much faster if he were to search alone. After communicating to us that he was going to leave us behind while he scouted for a new dwelling, he swiftly disappeared out of sight. My brother and I started a fire with the wood we had gathered while my capable mother soon appeared, wearing a pleased and satisfied smile. In her arms she carried a plentiful amount of fruit she had found for us to eat while we sat hidden among the boulders and patiently waited for my father's return.

Days had passed when suddenly I heard my brother's shouts alerting us that he had spotted our father trudging up the path. When my father reached us, he quickly communicated, with much excitement in his motions, that he had found us another cave. Indicating that the cave was on the mountain range across the valley, he made it clear that we must hurry if we hoped to reach it by nightfall. Gathering up our belongings, with a renewed eagerness we willingly followed him down the sharply sloping mountain to our new home.

Darkness had already fallen by the time we arrived at our destination. Setting down our heavy load inside what was now our new home, my brother and I quickly went in search of some fuel for our fire while our mother and father busily readied the cave for us to live in. Building a fire had always been the daily task for my brother and me ever since we were first taught how to make one. It kept us warm, provided light, and most important of all, now that we were lower on the mountain, it would drive away the dangerous predators and help to keep us safe.

There had been times when, during the building of a fire, I had wondered how our kind managed to survive before we knew how to use fire. My grandfather had once told me that when he was growing up, it was rare to see another of our breed. With the discovery of flint, and the knowledge of how it could be used to make fire and weapons, our kind had protection from predators and we were able to grow in numbers to where there were now several clans living in these mountains.

We lived a relatively peaceful life in the years after we moved to our new home. Never again were we subjected to the harsh winters we had been forced to endure while living in our mountaintop cave. Recently, however, the mighty mountain on which we now lived seemed to be angry with us. Strange rumbling noises could be heard coming from deep within it. In the last few days, the ground had been sporadically shaking beneath our feet. We had experienced this kind of shaking from time to time in the past several months, but the repetitive vibrations coming from underneath the ground had now become a daily and stronger occurrence. My family became anxious, for we were unable to understand what these changes meant for our future.

With all of us gathered outside the cave on a warm afternoon, we patiently watched as my mother prepared the one meal we ate each day. Suddenly my intensely sensitive father alerted us to the eerie silence that had befallen the mountain. Then the earth below our feet began to shake violently. So violently, in fact, that it became increasingly difficult for us to stand and we fell helplessly to our knees as the mountain exploded. ·The loud, startling sounds were deafening. The billowing cloud of smoke now vigorously spewing from the mountain's top turned our once-blue sky as black and dark as night.

The loss of the sun caused the temperature to drop sharply and the afternoon grew cold. Overtaken by fear, I looked to my father for some explanation of what was happening. The stunned expression on his face told me he had never experienced anything like this before.

Immobilized by fear, I observed my frightened mother crying hysterically, huddled up in a ball by the cave's entrance. My helpless father was on all fours, crawling frantically across the heaving ground, unsure of what to do. Huge rocks and boulders began falling from the sky, and narrowly missed striking us as we fearfully stumbled for the safety of our home. Cowering in the farthest corner of the cave, we were petrified by the mountain's growing discontent and the loud crashing noises from the shower of rocks outside.

We watched in disbelief and horror as the raining rocks and grey powdery substance began to cover the cave entrance, sealing our fate. Refusing to surrender, my father viciously clawed at the entrance in a last attempt to keep us from being buried alive, but his valiant efforts went unrewarded. Having admitted defeat, my father came to where we were huddled and sat alongside us.

We all knew we were about to die from the destructive force that was wreaking havoc outside the cave. In an effort to comfort us, my mother desperately held on to my brother and me. It was all she could think of to protect her ill-fated children. Death entered the cave in the form of a steaming, poisonous vapor. My throat tightened as the toxic gases penetrated and I could feel its grasp as it began to strangle my lungs. Choking uncontrollably, we labored to breathe for fresh air but it was no use. My mother was the first to die; my younger brother was the second. On the ground I could see my father writhing in pain and together we fought to stay alive with every last bit of strength we could hold onto, but soon our struggle ended and death accomplished what it had come to the cave to do.

The professor interrupted this event I was agonizingly reliving to ask, "What is your next experience?"

"We're all floating now," was my response.

"Where do you go?" the professor asked. "I don't know, I'm still trying to understand what just happened to me."

He instructed me: "Just go on then, and see what happens."

"We're traveling towards a light and it's

illuminatingly bright," I explained.

"Do you go together?"

"Yes. I'm watching my life pass by," I blurted to him.

"How do you feel as you watch your life fly by?"

"It was a rough life," I tell him. "Full of pain and struggle, but even though it was extremely challenging, I feel that I was good and I was loved."

The professor continued: "Tell me what happens next."

"It's extremely bright above me."

"What kind of place are you in?"

"I'm not really sure, but I am alone now." I no longer had a body, I explained to the professor, for I too was just a bright light.

Trust

My family from the cave must have had some other journey or life lesson to learn, because they had all moved on and I was alone. I was no longer in danger, but that did not stop me from worrying uncontrollably about my recent, traumatic death. The extremely distressing memories of that harrowing event consumed my every thought.

Because I had fought so passionately to stay alive, I was now obsessively revisiting what, if anything, we could have done differently that would have changed our fate. Maybe we shouldn't have run back into the cave, which created the perfect condition for suffocation by the gases that seeped in. Maybe we should have stayed on the other mountain and taken our chances with the harsh winter, instead of moving to a mountain that was troubled and angry. Concerned about my family and where they had gone, I could not shake this worry; my mind was a whirl of random, tornado-like thoughts, so much so that I could not find peace.

Then, miraculously, I heard a calm voice outside my own thoughts gently persuading me to end the anguish I was inflicting upon myself. I knew this encouragement was not coming from my own psyche because there was nothing peaceful about my thoughts. Soothing words continued until I was comforted enough to understand what was transpiring around me.

I was now caught in the midst of an astounding electrical storm. My young, strong body had been transformed into a ball of dazzling light that was alive with searing bolts of blue and white light that continually pulsated through me. This lively flow of energy, like constant lightning strikes, was being fed to me through a larger, more powerful light source high above me. The tormenting thoughts that had consumed me were now being exposed and responded to without my needing to actually express them. Each time a thought came, an equally strong lesson came from it that helped me to understand.

Sensing that I was in the presence of the original source of all energy and life throughout the entirety of time, I believed in that moment that I was experiencing God. The warm rays of light from this higher power were far-reaching, and I could feel the nurturing beams embracing me. Picture yourself lying on a beach with the sun directly above you. Your body fills with warmth as you quietly lie there, and the feeling is one of comfort. The rays from the sun are widespread and you can feel its energy. This was how I felt the whole time this warm light was embracing me, and it continued until finally I felt at one with the light.

My opened mind had shifted from obsessing over my recent death to calmly learning from this ultimate source of wisdom, which now shared its vast gifts of knowledge with me. A gentle voice penetrated my thoughts and let it be known that there was no need to be concerned about my death. It was patiently explained to me that the death of one's body was something that needed to be experienced in order for the growth of the soul to occur. It was also revealed that here in His presence, surrounded by His unconditional love, it was my time to grow and learn.

I was taught that "trust" was the lesson I had to learn. That whatever hardships I might face, I must trust that it is through adversity we learn our most valuable lessons. Coping with the loss of a loved one would be easier to accept if I learned to trust in my heart that the light was also preparing a truly meaningful awakening to enter into my life. This power conveyed to me that I worried too much. Trusting and believing in His words would lead to a future that never needed to be worried about.

I understood that it was for me to learn that life is full of experiences, and whether those experiences are positive or negative, they are necessary to our soul's journey and without them we cannot learn from life to life. Fully embrace life and all it has to offer, my teacher impressed upon me, be truly accepting of the lessons you've been given, and you will find peace and everlasting love. I felt as if the words, "trust that I am being guided, trust that I am being protected" were being written upon my soul. Over and over again the message of "trust me" was repeated. It continued until I was finally made to understand.

The magnificent light suddenly disappeared

as I heard the professor tell me our time was up for the day, and he returned me back to the present. After a few minutes, my grogginess began to wane and the professor and I engaged in a discussion about the three lives I had just relived: my outgoing life as an adventurous explorer, the death of my champion horse and the solitary life that followed, and my surprising life and death as a young caveman.

I told the professor that out of those three lives, the personality I felt I could most closely relate to was that of John Powell's. The captain possessed a gregarious, competitive nature and he took pleasure in easing his crew's worries by making them laugh. As the leader of his seafaring group of men, he would enthusiastically gather everyone together for some sword fighting endeavors or the retelling of a humorous tale or two.

In my current life, I too am called upon to

entertain friends and family with my many true-to-life tales. Almost all my life, because of my fun, outgoing nature, my friends have frequently requested that I formulate some kind of enjoyable activities for them. Over the years, my confidence in myself has drawn numerous people to me from all walks of life. My personality has made me well liked among the many people that I have encountered. The similarities of my and John Powell's extrovert personalities had clearly caught my attention while reflecting on this past life story.

At the end of his meaningful life, John Powell had expressed his most sincere love for the valued life he had lived. Possessing that same heartfelt love for my current life, I can honestly and openly picture myself reflecting on the significance of my life, much as he had done right before his passing. I have lived a life full of love, pleasure, heartache, and the mundane, and just like John Powell, I too will be sad to leave this life behind.

The professor and I went on to discuss the fact that there were some parallels in the feelings that I had experienced, too. When I was envisioning my life as Beth and my beloved horse died after severely injuring his leg, the emotional pain I felt was indescribable. I felt that same level of pain in my current lifetime when I lost my much-loved husband Steve in a horrible automobile accident. Both deaths were sudden and tragic, and the deep feelings of anguish I experienced in both lives seemed nearly identical. When the professor and I had finished with our short analysis, I left his office feeling tired and drained.

Though I harbored a desire to learn as much as possible about any past lives I might have experienced, I had to admit that I found these visits to be time-consuming and exhausting. By the time I returned to the professor's office the following week, I had already made up my mind that this visit would be my last (a decision I later regretted). Because I did not return for my final two sessions,

189

the professor did not send me a tape of my last visit.

As the professor performed his hypnotic routine on me for the last time, I found myself in the same long hallway I had been to twice before. Searching in earnest for the door that yearned to be opened, I entered the one that called out to me and without any hesitation I stepped into my next life.

The Middle Ages

Rapidly evolving images began to manifest inside my captivated mind. By focusing intensely, I was able to communicate to the professor that I saw myself standing in an open, arched doorway made of stones. Once again I found myself to be a young man, who looked to be somewhere in his late twenties. I told the professor that I was of average height, with a thin, muscular build and brown, wavy, shoulder-length hair.

Upon entering the large royal banquet hall, my gaze was immediately drawn upward towards its magnificent, vaulted, beamed ceiling and the somewhat impressive stained-glass windows, each depicting the illustration of a jeweled-encrusted crown resting on top of an aristocratic family crest.

Long dining tables, draped with white linen cloths, lay stretched out before me. Dangling directly over the tables were illuminating candles, glowing from their perch atop wooden cross-shaped chandeliers that had been suspended from the ceiling by a tied-down rope. The gray stone walls surrounding me would have given the room a dreary feeling, if it were not for a few mounted deer head trophies and the intricately woven wall hangings that narrated stories of brave knights in battle. An intense fire burning in a capacious hearth off to the right of me warmed the otherwise cold interior.

I had positioned myself off to one side of the wide doorway and slightly out of sight because I was feeling unwelcome. I witnessed about two dozen or so guests gluttonously dining on a lavish feast of what looked to be whole seasoned lamb legs, assorted fresh fruits, and some crispy root vegetables. These privileged and pampered individuals were being catered to by a handful of submissive servants, who indulged their every whim. The chairs the guests sat in had very high, pointed backs; so high, in fact, that from where I stood I could only see the tips of the women's cone-shaped hats.

As I inched my way towards the tables to have a closer look, I noticed that the hats resembled dunce caps, except that they were topped with high-quality lace that draped down over the women's shoulders. The men, who were much more elegantly dressed then the women, wore doublets with sewn-on rubies and emeralds, and a pair of fancy breeches.

Prominently positioned at the head of the main table was the regal-looking host of this night's extravagance. I was immediately taken aback by the spectacle of this rather obese man who was uncomfortably stuffed into the elaborately carved, throne-like chair in which he sat. He wore a round, reddish-brown felt hat that allowed shoots of gray hair to protrude from the sides of his head. A scruffy gray beard framed his bloated, red-veined, double-chinned face. He was tightly wrapped in an ornate rust-colored silk robe, trimmed with ermine fur that barely covered his massive gut. To complete his look, he was draped in gold chains, studded with jewels, and on his chubby hands he wore rings that easily cost a knight's annual salary.

This eminent figure was the king of this grand castle, and his well-to-do guests seated at the tables had been invited here for a night of lively merrymaking and to be entertained by me and my two music-making best friends, who had just arrived.

My friends and I were considerably skilled traveling minstrels. As a group, we composed our own ballads and sang songs that told detailed stories, real or imaginary, about distant places of interest or past noteworthy events. We were well known throughout the neighboring countryside as unbelievably talented musicians. The king was quite aware of our stellar reputation and had requested our band to play for him on a number of occasions.

I was about to play a lute, a plucked musical instrument that was flat, with a pear-shaped body. Another member's instrument was a tambour, a shallow drum, and the smallest and skinniest member of the group played a psaltery, a small, solid, wooden stringed instrument that was shaped like a triangle.

The three of us were hardly dressed for tonight's banquet, as we were wearing the only clothes we possessed. We wore tights, knee-high suede boots, and crudely-shaped tunics tied at the waist by rope belts. Although it was the customary style worn by the local commoners, it looked extremely awkward on my short, skinny friend with his toothpick-like legs.

We had been summoned here to dutifully entertain; nevertheless, we were not very fond of this feudal king. In fact, down the hill in the village where we dwelled, all who lived there hated this malevolent monarch because of his selfish and greedy ways. His towering, reinforced fortress, which sat on the edge of a high, steep cliff and overlooked the vast ocean below, concealed his decadent lifestyle. Access to his private domain with its lavish, lush, designed-to-impress gardens was restricted and tightly controlled. His days were surrounded by splendor, while for many years countless villagers within his territory had suffered a tremendous toll under his rule.

The local peasants were callously forced to work the fertile land while earning meager wages to produce the food and textiles the king and his manor required. The townspeople were heavily taxed and were required to relinquish almost all of what was harvested to this unscrupulous ruler.

Under his strict control, not the fish in the sea nor the deer that roamed the large, dense forest belonged to the people. A severe punishment was delivered to anyone caught hunting wildlife belonging to the king without his exclusive permission. Under this shameful system, while the king and his chosen few indulged in great wealth and an overabundance of food, his people suffered needlessly from a lack of material goods and nourishment.

To be the entertainment for this king was definitely a huge moral struggle for us. Each time we performed, we had to pretend we held this callous tyrant in the highest regard. But deep down in our hearts, we despised his exploitation of us and of all the people who lived under his control. Drunk with power, this cruel and heartless man felt that playing for him at his gatherings should be an honor, and because of this he did not pay us our usual fee.

This night would be no different. In fact, as we wandered amid the dining tables playing our instruments and singing upbeat melodies, we watched in disgust as the guests mindlessly overindulged in food and drink. We painfully listened as they mocked us and laughed at our tiny village's misfortune. Forced to endure their cutting remarks, we listened as they hard-heartedly referred to our family and friends as "those poor disgusting little peasants down the hill." The more we heard their malicious talk, the angrier we became. So offensive were their comments that it took every bit of strength we had to control our emotions. During a break, we decided that we had had enough. No longer could we stand idly by and take this oppressive behavior anymore. Right there, among our soon-to-be prey, we plotted our revenge.

Together, we conspired to pilfer some of the king's precious possessions. Because the king and his guests had become quite intoxicated, we felt certain that the treasures that lay before us would be easy pickings. We felt overly confident that none of these thoughtless nobles would be the least bit suspicious of us, or even take notice if we left that evening with some of the king's ill-gotten gains.

The first time we stole valuable items from the castle, it was effortless and trouble-free. My fast-thinking friends filled the bags that usually held their instruments with spices, jugs of wine, and leftover food. I was a little bolder, taking several porcelain bowls, a couple of golden, jewel-encrusted goblets, and anything I thought would be valuable. That night, as we departed across the drawbridge, carrying our heavy load, none of the many armored guards tried to stop us. Once we had made it to the false safety of the other side, we all let out a huge sigh of relief. After a couple of nervous days passed, it was just as we had suspected: no one from the castle had noticed that their precious items had disappeared.

In the weeks that followed, we traveled to a large, populated town far enough away from the castle to elude suspicion. It was there that we were able to trade some of the king's goods for rye flour and oats — enough to provide some relief to the sick and famished people in our village. Taking a huge risk, we also bartered for crop seeds so our people could secretly grow and tend their own separate harvests. The three of us knew what we were doing was a dangerous act, but it was a gamble we were willing to take.

As time passed and our unshakable hatred for everything this king stood for increased, the three of us rebelliously took on what we believed was our God-given mission. We felt it was up to us to bring some dignity to the people we cared for. It was the least we could do, as the king had no intention of ever showing empathy or compassion for the conditions the people were living in. The gratitude showered upon us by the townspeople only made us more determined to do the right thing. Because of what the three of us were willing to sacrifice, we had become admired and respected by one and all for our staunch bravery.

Over a period of time, with every compulsory invitation to entertain the king and his chosen few, we continued to plunder his coveted goods. Alas, as fate would have it, one day we were caught red-handed by the king himself as we were stuffing some of his valuable possessions into our instrument bags. As he walked aggressively towards us, using his gold-and-onyx walking stick to aid his massive frame, we could tell by his flaring nostrils and fiery-red, spider-veined cheeks that he was enraged. Menacing, armor-clad guards with swords and shields blocked the passageway that could have allowed our escape. Sensing that our fate had been sealed, the three of us stood petrified at the thought of what cruel punishment this heartless king would deem suitable.

The incensed king was fully aware that this was not the first time we had stolen from him, a crime already severe enough, and that we had also defiantly traded his personal effects to help the townspeople to better themselves. With contempt in his voice, he ruled right then and there that a slow, painful death by starvation would be the only just punishment for our treasonous crimes. Without delay, the king had us banished to dark and dreary cells deep below the castle.

The dungeon was accessed through damp, narrow, winding passageways, which served to muffle the agonizing cries of tortured victims from the inhabitants of the castle. While being forcefully dragged past the gated cells, I could sense the suffering and anguish of all the unfortunate unknowns who had been brought here to die.

Dread saturated my entire body as I

struggled to look behind me at my two thrashing friends, who were now pleading for mercy. Momentarily I was able to catch a glimpse of the same anguished look of intense fear on their faces that I was feeling in that moment.

Taken to the same small, barren room, we bravely made one last attempt to save ourselves by grabbing and then forcefully pushing and punching the guards in hopes of freeing ourselves, but it was of no use. We were swiftly beaten into submission and quickly shackled side-by-side to the stone wall. Not being satisfied with just leaving us there, bruised and battered, the guards spat on us and kicked dirt in our faces before turning to leave us to our merciless fate. The loud clang of the iron gate as it was slammed shut and the fading footsteps of the brutal guards as they vanished from sight were the last sounds we ever heard from the outside world. Never again did we see another soul.

At first, in a refusal to just lay there and die,

we were full of optimism and the unrealistic hope that the townspeople, out of gratitude for all we had done for them, would storm the castle and rescue us. But several days later all of our misplaced confidence faded and we reluctantly surrendered to our fate. We had come to understand and accept that any endeavor the townspeople attempted on our behalf would have only resulted in them sharing our fate.

Declaring to ourselves that even though we had no hope, we would have no fear, we each solemnly vowed to one another to be brave until the bitter end. With the remaining time we had left, we evoked memories of the enjoyable times we had shared growing up, the pleasurable times spent writing ballads and playing our music, and most importantly, how much we were going to miss our families. Even though we knew the stealing was wrong, we had done it for all the right reasons, and we were going to die having no regrets.

Unfortunately for the three of us, death could not come fast enough. Because we were severely dehydrated, all movement became painful. The excruciating pains in our stomach from lack of nourishment led to delirium. In our last days we appealed to God for compassion and mercy, but our anguished pleas went unrequited. Finally, one by one we slipped into deep comas that mercifully ended our reign of agony. The only solace we had in our final days was that we remained together, loyal friends until the very end.

The Print Shop

In the depths of that cold, dark dungeon, almost at the same exact moment, my musical friends and I gasped our last dying breath of that lifetime. And then, before our souls even had a chance to rise, in an instant the three of us were rapidly whisked away and just as suddenly, we materialized inside our mother's nurturing womb. Though it seemed unbelievable, our emotional bond for one another had been so powerful that we were now about to embark on a new life together.

Abruptly, I began to sense that our current, comforting conditions were about to take a turn for the worse. Somehow, I could feel my mother's distressing and exhausted struggle through her voice as she frantically screamed in anguish. To her, this birth felt abnormally different from the first five births she had gone through. Those children gave her pain, but nothing like what she was experiencing while giving birth to us triplets. Bleeding heavily, my mother grew weaker as she managed to give birth to me and my brothers — the one who had been my small and delicate friend in my last life did not survive the birth. My mother too was now struggling to survive, and in the end she did not live.

Our father, who stood supportively by our mother's bedside throughout the whole excruciating ordeal, holding her hand, encouraging her to fight, was now devastated by this cruel turn of events. Feeling forlorn after having just lost the only woman he had ever truly loved, he was taken aback by the reality of the situation and the fact that he had now been left alone with two additional mouths to feed. Overwhelmed and heartbroken, our father was too weak-willed to handle the emotional and financial burden of this tragedy and he selfishly sent us to live with our maternal grandmother, who resided in the majestic mountains surrounding the town.

Unfortunately for my brother and me, our childhood years were deficient in any kind of emotional or physical relationship with our father and our five siblings. Begrudgingly, once or twice a year our neglectful father would make a woeful effort to trek up the mountainside to our home and drop off some used clothing that our older brothers had outgrown. At all times staying for only a short, dispassionate visit, the antsy outsider would in no time retreat from his obligatory mission and quickly scurry his way down the mountain path to his own life.

Throughout our father's long absences, my brother and I would often carefully consider the long-rumored notion whispered among the people living on the mountain that he in some way held us accountable for the death of our mother. This emotionally injured man had never fully recovered from the passing of his beloved wife, and perhaps that was why for years he chose to distance himself from the two of us. Thoughts that our father could harbor such ill feelings against his own offspring frequently haunted us both.

My brother and I, wanting to resolve the constant conflict we carried within, unburdened our feelings to our prudent grandmother. We revealed to her our knowledge of the idle speculations and asked if she too thought our mother's untimely death, caused by our difficult birth, was why we never saw our father. Our grandmother harshly stated that those kind of negative thoughts and opinions about our father rejecting us because of the loss of his wife were completely unreasonable. She steadfastly insisted that our father loved us very much, and that he was just a busy man, working hard to raise the other children. She further insisted, in an unyielding tone, that he was not the kind of man to carry resentment in his heart and if he could, he would undoubtedly visit us more.

Over time we reluctantly accepted our grandmother's opinion, deciding to forgive our father's transgressions and simply move on. Leaving the negative past behind, we chose to live in the moment and be thankful for the life our loving grandmother had been able to provide for us.

Ours was a pleasant life. Our modest dwelling had floors made of hardened earth and a thatched roof that was strong and secure. Inside the cottage, our unpretentious, well-crafted furniture was basic but useful. We had two sturdy benches, a table with chairs, and a large wooden chest for storage, and we each slept on a mattress stuffed with straw that lay on ropes strung across a solid wooden frame.

For decades our grandmother had resided in the tiny mountaintop abode with its breathtakingly beautiful views of mountain peaks and the charming rustic town nestled below. The green meadows of the low-lying valleys, with their patches of wildflowers, stretched below us as far as the eye could see and in the winter, the snow covering the peaks sat like whipped cream on top of an ice cream sundae.

Years of living with our nurturing grandmother had taught us to be reliable and self-sufficient. We were skilled at cultivating the land and tending to the livestock that provided us with a variety of fresh food and other useful products. We had readily learned the strict discipline needed to wake up with the roosters and the patience to tend to our sometimes-mischievous goats. Outdoors in the cool breeze of autumn days, my brother and I would laboriously gather and chop enough wood to last us through entire cold seasons. Our rewards for this physically exertive effort were strong, muscular bodies and warm, comfortable winters.

My brother and I were also creative at crafting tools and constructing furniture, like the items we had built for our grandmother's house. We could even knit our own warm sweaters from the soft wooly undercoat that the goats grew in the wintertime. In order for our grandmother to have money for feed and such, several times a year we would take our best goods to town and sell them with much success.

As we grew up, our astute grandmother taught us the benefits of having a strong work ethic, and she made sure that we had all the specific knowledge needed to survive a life in the rugged mountains. Wanting us to have book knowledge as well, four days a week our grandmother saw to it that we attended the primary school in town. Both my brother and I were regarded by many as quick learners and highly intelligent students, which made both our grandmother and our teachers proud.

As the years passed and we grew into adulthood, we were sad to see our once-vibrant grandmother age to the point where she was no longer able to engage in her daily routines. We made her final years happy in the best way we knew how. Sadly, by the time we had reached our mid-twenties, our beloved grandmother had peacefully passed away in her sleep.

Our strong belief that God would be waiting with open arms to lovingly welcome this saintly woman home helped to ease our intense sorrow. With a few of our longtime neighbors attending, we buried the only woman we had ever loved on a wildflower-covered hillside overlooking her beloved homestead. Grandmother's name, carved into a large flat rock by my own powerful hands, served as her grave marker.

A couple of her lady friends gently positioned beautifully arranged bouquets of freshly picked flowers around the marker as a tribute to this wonderful, benevolent woman. All of us attending believed it would have been something that she would have relished. And it was of no surprise to anyone present that our uninterested father did not bother to attend.

I gave a small speech on behalf of my brother and myself, and stated how deeply saddened we were to have lost the greatest influence we had known in our life so far. I further expressed that we had found some solace in the fact that because of our grandmother's strength and endurance, she had left the legacy of two happy, intelligent, and well-behaved young men. Forever and immensely grateful to our grandmother for giving us a loving and secure upbringing, we vowed to continue to make her proud in every endeavor we pursued.

My brother and I remained living in our home for a few more years, until there came a point in time when we instinctively knew that it would be best for us to move on. With the passing of our mentor and emotional nurturer, there was no longer a purpose or a desire to stay. Needing to make use of the excellent schooling we had been given, we both agreed to no longer waste our gift of knowledge by tending to goats and chickens.

After selling our dearly departed grandmother's home, animals and all, we gathered up all of our belongings and made our way down the mountain path towards a new beginning in town. As our luck would have it, on that very first day, we found a small room to rent in the center of town while we looked for a more permanent place to live. We were not interested in finding any old place, but instead we desired a home that would be just the right fit for us and for our new life.

In no time, to our satisfaction, we ran across a

quaint little print shop for sale, which had living quarters on the second floor. It was perfect. The shop had an inviting appearance thanks to windows covered by brown shutters, and to the variety of colorful flowers blossoming in wooden boxes that hung outside the second-story windows.

Inside, we found numerous printers' tools mounted neatly on a wall. We took special notice of the solid, wood-base printing press that measured five feet long, three feet wide, and seven feet tall; we were intrigued by its moveable workings. Accompanying the large press were cases of cast-metal type pieces and typeset matter that made this shop even more enticing.

With the money we had received from the sale of our grandmother's home and with the small inheritance that she had bequeathed to us, we were able to buy that pleasant print shop. My brother and I were elated about owning our own business and we went to work immediately, teaching ourselves every intricate detail there was to learn about our new trade. As we taught ourselves the skillful art of arranging type into pages and the delicate inking process, we soon learned that the rearrangement of the letters each time a new page was to be printed would be a long and laborious task.

For hours on end we talked passionately about how we were going to start a town newspaper — something never before seen in these parts — and what types of stories we would print. Our first mission was to acquire as much information as we could about the history of the town and to form personal connections with the people who resided there. Our goal was to use every opportunity we could to learn and grow and then, in turn, to share our experiences with others.

We scheduled question-and-answer sessions with as many people as possible. This was easy, as we were already known and well-liked in town. Our idea of a town newspaper that would include such features as economic conditions, social customs, and human interest stories was very well received, which further fueled our ambitions.

There was a welcoming tavern in the middle of town that was the focal point of this community. Hand-painted on a sign hanging on a pole directly above the door was an illustration of a bell tower, the bar's only identifying mark. The tavern's windows were frosted glass to obscure the patrons from the passersby on the street. Comfortable and unassuming, with a great clientele mix of young and old, it was the kind of place where people gathered to gossip, share stories about their lives, or just relax after a long, hard day.

This local watering hole had its usual characters, including my brother and me, and the occasional weary traveler passing through town. Wine and food were sold there, but what the people really enjoyed was the ale, which the bar owner had a matchless talent for brewing. As the evening wore on and more alcohol was consumed, the livelier the stories got. The friendly, generous treatment the proprietor offered to his guests was so relaxing and pleasing that by the time the night was over, everyone was in good spirits and a jovial time was had by all. At the end of the night, we would bid our farewells and sure enough, when the next night rolled around, everyone could be found at that welcoming bar. It had become obvious to my brother and me that this popular lair would be the perfect location for gathering the substantive and never-ending material needed for our forthcoming newspaper stories.

At first, our subjects were not quick to reveal private information that would be documented for all to see. Persuading them took some time, but eventually we were able to gain their trust and support. My brother and I were careful to only write about their personal experiences in a positive light, and never to embarrass or alienate anyone.

One of our foremost true-life stories had come from the good-natured tavern owner himself, who was gracious enough to allow us to interview him. His only condition was that he read the article before it went to print, and my brother and I agreed. The story revolved around his family's financial struggles in the early days of owning the Bell Tower bar, and how it had grown into the openhearted social setting that it was today. We quoted him saying, "The bar's success is due to the people of this town. We look after them and they look after us."

We interviewed the patrons and asked them to comment on their own experiences in the bar, and what made them come back day after day. The bar owner was very clever about what he wanted us to publish about him. He knew that just the right wording could bring him more business success. His article was revised many times before we were able to get his approval. The long-awaited story of the well-respected bar owner was finally ready for print.

The day it was announced that the first newspapers were about to be rolled off the press, a small, excited crowd gathered outside the print shop door. Pleasantly surprised at how eager people were to purchase the paper, we feverishly worked to fulfill their demand. Once news had spread about the story we had published, the bar owner became quite a celebrity in town, and the bar began to attract even more visitors than ever before. My brother and I were extremely satisfied with the desired outcome and could not have predicted what would happen next.

Visiting the bar the week the article was published, we found that our own popularity had increased and that our newspaper was the main topic of conversation. Random people began stopping by the print shop, offering to tell my brother and me about their life stories in hope that we would write about them in our paper. Others asked if we could put their notices of business, births, deaths, and anything else they could conjure up to print just so they too could be in our newspaper. Before long, my brother and I had become inundated with stories to publish. As we labored night and day to keep up with the demand, we felt certain our beloved grandmother was watching over us, proud that our dream to create a successful newspaper was rapidly coming to fruition.

The most fascinating part of this bold undertaking came a month or two later, when a visitor from out of town took the first issue of our paper with him on his journey home. In no time, people from neighboring towns had come in search of the Bell Tower bar to see if the splendidly written story was true. As my brother and I chatted with the newcomers, it was obvious that their other reason for coming here was to purchase several copies of our paper to take back home. It was truly more than my brother and I would have dreamed possible. The demand for our newspaper had increased to the point that we could no longer conduct daily operations by ourselves; we needed help and we needed someone quickly.

With the intent of hiring several strong, able-bodied young men to help with the now-high print volume and the distribution end of the business, we hung a "Help wanted" sign in the print shop window. Out of the blue, one of the very first men to apply turned out to be our nephew, the son of one of our older, now-deceased brothers. To our amazement, he revealed to us that while he was growing up, his grandfather (also now deceased) had shared with him and the other children brief stories about the two of us, our grandmother, and the life we had lived on the old homestead, but our nephew had never really understood why we had never met.

He told us that after he had read our extraordinarily well-written newspaper, it made him curious and excited about the process of printing, and that he would be truly grateful for the opportunity to work with us. Flattered by his remarks and wanting a relationship with our newfound nephew, we took him under our wing and taught him all things necessary to run a successful printing business. In exchange, he willingly shared with us all the knowledge he had about our absentee father and the family we had never known.

This young man was hard-working and as devoted to the business as my brother and I were. Our nephew turned out to be a godsend and a perfect fit for the job. Many late nights after a hard day's work were spent upstairs in our tiny kitchen above the print shop. Dining on a hot meal and swigging from a jug of ale, we often laughed and occasionally choked back a tear or two as he shared family memories with us.

My brother and I were pleased to once again

have someone in our life who was family. We now had the opportunity to teach and guide this young man, much in the same way that our grandmother had done for us so many years ago, and this brought great joy into our lives. Over time we were introduced to other family members as well, and soon these kind souls were inviting us to supper and including us in some of their holiday activities.

Because the printing press was a relatively new concept for this time period and the region in which we lived, it was thought to be more of a novelty than anything else. Before we bought the shop, our press had been used to reprint manuscripts and bestselling books of the day.

Because of our relentless determination, it truly was the beginning of distributing imaginative and useful information that went beyond our small village and into the neighboring towns.

To keep our newspaper's stories fresh and interesting, two of our newly hired assistants were sent roving from one town to another, reporting on upcoming events, unusual facts, and human interest stories for the curious folks back home. Through our newspaper, our town and the neighboring towns soon felt a beneficial social and economic connection.

As time passed, our town's economy grew and my brother and I became highly respected and quite successful. Much of the money we had earned we gave back generously to the town that had been so good to us. One of the first projects we chose to fund was the upgrading of the tiny schoolhouse where my brother and I had received our outstanding education. As a show of gratitude, a decorative fountain dedicated in our honor was erected in the middle of town.

With my brother and I being so greatly devoted to our business, years passed quickly; we never really settled down long enough to even think about getting married or having families of our own. On many occasions, well-meaning townsfolk would make a good-hearted effort to set the two of us up with very lovely and proper young ladies. However, the connection never really grew into anything more than friendship. At first it seemed odd to almost everyone that two young, good-looking men would have no real desire to marry, but once they got to know us better, they understood and accepted our choice.

Perhaps our mother's death when we were so young and our life with our widowed grandmother kept us away from forming any truly intimate relationships. Growing up without the knowledge or examples of what a significant relationship was all about, we didn't feel it was necessary for a full life. As my brother and I grew older and we were considered past the marrying age, the well-meaning matchmaking began to subside. It had become obvious to all that our one true love had been and would always be publishing and the expansion of our newspaper business.

As we advanced into old age, our once-strong bodies began to betray us and our once-sharp minds became forgetful. Eventually, we had no choice but to declare defeat and hand over the business to our deserving nephew. From our living quarters upstairs we could hear the delightful clanging sounds of the printing press cranking out its daily lot. Unable to get around as we once did, we still managed to inch our way downstairs every day with the hope that we might somehow be needed.

The remaining stages of our well-lived lives were happy and remarkably content, though we were now homebound above our beloved print shop. Loving friends and caring acquaintances stopped by to hear us retell the thought-provoking stories of our accomplished lives. And just as at the end of our last life, once again my brother and I were together at the end; although this time we were rewarded with a much more peaceful ending.

I don't remember what the professor and I discussed at the end of this session, but I'm almost positive he would have pointed out the astonishing recall of when my musician friends and I died at the same time and were immediately reborn as triplets. What an amazing thought to consider.

What I had learned from my last session was that I had carried over into this life the same passion for justice as I'd had during my life as a traveling minstrel. During the final years of my life in the Middle Ages, I was focused on making sure that the less fortunate had what they deserved, regardless of the consequences. In the later years of my current life, I have become a bit of an activist with a strong belief in fairness and equality. I have always had compassion and empathy for others, and the courage to strongly voice my opinion when I feel someone is being treated unfairly.

I also believe that my life as a printer, writer, and editor may have sparked my desire to write the heartfelt story you're now reading.

This Life

My own story began in 1954, when I was born Julie Marie Douat at O'Connor Hospital in San Jose, California. From the spirited stories I heard my relatives tell while I was growing up, my parents were very excited to see me the day I was born. They used to say emphatically to all who would listen that I was the precious little girl my Mom and Dad had been waiting for. My family at the time of my birth consisted of my caring Mom, my hardworking Dad, and my three playful brothers: Bob (age five), Steve (age four), and Denis (age two).

My parents, both born and raised in San Jose and growing up less then a mile apart from each other, first met on a blind date that had been arranged by a few of their mutual friends. My mother, a slender beauty with an infectious smile, and my handsome father, who could have easily been mistaken for a young Jimmy Stewart, instantly knew that the closeness they felt meant that they were to be together forever. After a short courtship, they were married at St. Leo's, a local Catholic church, and remained very much in love and devoted to one another throughout their entire fifty-nine years of marriage.

A stay-at-home mom like most women of that time period, my mother believed strongly that it was her job to teach us good manners and, most importantly, instill in us the difference between right and wrong.

Growing up, my parents' number-one priority was to make sure that the family was always well fed, no matter how little money we had. In my Civil War past life, my parents and I died because of a lack of food; I remember making the connection during the session that those parents were also my parents in this life. It made me wonder if my parents had carried over their past life experience with a lack of food into their current life.

My sometimes light-hearted Mom possessed a fun side that she used to entertain us kids. As she merrily called out, "It's story time," we willingly gathered on the floor around her feet while she made herself comfortable in her big, green, overstuffed chair. Because we were so captivated, we didn't move; we listened intently as she vivaciously read our top pick from her collection of popular children's books. *Charlie and the Chocolate Factory* was our all-time favorite story, which she was compelled to read by popular request on multiple occasions.

Singing songs was another one of my mother's enjoyable qualities. Often in the morning hours, while we were snuggled in our beds, my mother would appear in our rooms and awaken us by singing, "You are my sunshine, my only sunshine" or "Wake up sleepy head, get up, get out of bed."

Raising several lively children could at times be quite challenging, so one of Mom's responsibilities was that of the steadfast disciplinarian (just like my authoritarian Civil War mother). It was a job she did quite well, I might add. She always managed to keep us in our place with a few firm words and a scornful look.

Being the first girl born, I was somewhat of a Daddy's girl (like Annabelle was to her father), so naturally he was the parent I was closest to while growing up. My Dad was a busy man, as Annabelle's father had been. In both of our lives we longed to spend much more quality time with the fathers we adored.

My father was employed at Greenlee's, a local bakery near our house, and was either working long, laborious hours, or catching up on his much-needed sleep. Dad made a living as a baker, for he had a natural talent for decorating cakes. What he earned was not a doctor's salary by any means, but enough for us to get by on comfortably, even though with the birth of my sisters Cheryl and Diane, there were now six children to feed and care for.

My parents had a special type of admiring relationship, in which where they could never get enough of each other's love and affection. They were always hugging and smooching, and sometimes my Dad would chase my Mom around the house trying to pinch her bottom while she yelled, "Honey, stop that!" Frankly, it was embarrassing at times for all of us, especially when some of the neighborhood kids were over at our house playing. Theirs was an enduring love that had traveled through lifetimes, and it wasn't until we children had gotten older that we were able to truly appreciate it; maybe you could even say that we were all a little envious of the loving relationship our parents had.

We lived in a charming little neighborhood on a small, tree-lined street far away from any traffic that you might experience living in a big, noisy city. On patriotic holidays, our all-American street with its well-kept homes and a flagpole on every house could have easily passed for a scene straight out of a Norman Rockwell painting.

In the fifties and sixties it was not uncommon for most married couples to have large families, so it wasn't surprising to anyone that there were fifteen children living in three different homes at one end of our tiny street. Lucky for us, this allowed us to have our own football and baseball teams. You could find us out playing in the middle of the street almost every day after school and on weekends.

Before reflecting on my hypnosis experience with the professor, I hadn't given much thought as to how a person's current life would play into any of their past lives. Could it be as simple as kids loving to play in the street, I thought to myself, or maybe what a person lacks in one life, he or she gains in another. The professor and I had contemplated during one of our sessions that when I died prematurely in my life as Kathy, perhaps my reward for being a good person in that life was that in this life, I would have the freedom to play out in the street whenever I wanted, to have a loving father who was present, and to have a mother able to stay home and take care of me. It almost felt like my soul had evolved a bit in this regard, because I was able to experience in this life that which I could not in a prior existence.

During the session, I also told the professor

about something else I thought was fascinatingly strange. Our childhood home was located behind a large, abandoned, Colonial-style mansion that was run down and very much resembled my Civil War home at the time of my death as Annabelle Conner. Was it merely a coincidence, or did my parents subconscious past life memories attract them to our house behind the mansion?

The backyard of my childhood home was separated from a huge cherry orchard by a rather tall chain-link fence. Mixed in between the trees for as far as we could see were yellow-flowering mustard greens that grew as high as the top of our shoulders. Beyond the still and quiet orchard, the mysterious but magnificent, thirty-two-room, abandoned mansion lay hidden among tall trees and overgrown brush.

Every day on our way home from school, my siblings and I would walk down the historic tree-lined street known as the "Alameda." The street was originally built around 1795 by Native Americans living at Mission Santa Clara to link the mission with the El Pueblo de San Jose de Guadalupe (San Jose). In later years the street was best known for its many stately mansions, and as we made our way past the vacant, forbidden estate, we grew ever more interested as to what kind of unforeseen secrets it held within.

One day my curious brothers cut a man-size hole in the chain-link fence so that they could go on an exploratory mission through the orchard in a daring attempt to reach the mansion. Each time they would pass through the hole, my brothers silently hoped and prayed that today would not be the day they'd get caught trespassing by the watchful caretaker and his very large bull mastiff dog that would sometimes show up unexpectedly.

I was probably around seven years old when my brothers decided I was old enough and begrudgingly allowed me to tag along. I was thrilled. I idolized my older brothers and loved to mimic whatever they would do. At this point, for some unknown reason, the dutiful caretaker and his trusty companion had stopped coming. Now the stately home and surrounding grounds were ours to explore freely for our amusement. On our carefree way to the mansion, we couldn't resist creeping and crawling among the tall mustard greens as it was so easy to hide in them. That was half the fun of our investigative adventure.

The grand and imposing mansion, intentionally built so that it nestled among a grove of tall redwood trees, must have been quite a beautiful and pleasing home back in its day. As I recall, there were several ornate cement ponds positioned around the property to enhance the beauty of the home, and at the end of the long dirt driveway sat a six-door carriage house. Situated behind the house were a large, rectangular, cement swimming pool and a small, private, domed chapel that could have easily sat around fifty or so people.

Inside the majestic home, an elegantly designed grand staircase (like the one Annabelle had gracefully descended on the night of the celebration) led from the second floor with its many bedrooms down to the oversized, marble-floored foyer. Throughout the years I often wondered why someone would have just walked away and abandoned such a beautiful home.

Together with my brothers and a few of the other kids on our street, we always traveled in a pack. No one dared enter the spooky mansion alone. Even though the sunlight beaming through the many windows lit the inside enough for us to see, the mansion was large in its emptiness and just creepy enough that any one of us would be scared by the whispering echoes that occurred from the slightest of noises.

Once inside our destination, our mission was to search for valuables and artifacts. We meticulously examined every room, upstairs and down, for some kind of trap door or secret passageway that we were sure would lead us to hidden treasure that would make us all rich. But all I remember us finding was a hand-painted clay mold of an Egyptian man's face, and some old glass bottles — things that hardly brought us the wealth we were so hoping for.

Oddly, one night when I was ten years old, I had a dream that the impressive old mansion had caught on fire. In this dream I saw myself standing behind the house, watching as fierce flames and black smoke poured from shattered windows on the second floor. This vision was so vivid and felt so real that I remember, upon awakening, being extremely anxious and bothered by it.

That same morning, our great-aunt Aggie came by and took my brothers and me out for a weekend breakfast, something she loved to do. On our way back home we were surprised to see numerous fire trucks, with their red lights flashing, blocking the streets to our home. We all shouted cries of disbelief when we realized that the long-forsaken mansion was fully engulfed in flames. I remembered my dream and told anyone who would listen that I had just dreamed of this.

I suppose that a dream doesn't hold much clout when you're ten years old, because my brothers just made fun of me and my vision, and no matter how hard I tried to get someone to listen, no one believed me. I was frustrated that I hadn't shared my premonition with anyone before the fire, but I hadn't known that it would actually happen.

I have never forgotten that dream and the strange feeling that my dream had told me about something that was about to happen. It was one of those curious moments in life that makes someone wonder about the ability to predict future events. Some people embrace their gift of intuition and nurture it, and some people squelch it to ensure they are considered "normal." As I grew older, I continued to have dreams and thoughts about future events that sometimes came true; however, I quickly learned what I should and shouldn't share with some people due to their responses. I learned to keep my thoughts to myself.

When I was eight, my parents made the decision to send my brothers and me to St. Leo's, a Catholic school a few blocks from our home. This was a hard adjustment for me, and I was not at all happy with the change. Even though I had only been attending Hester Elementary for two years, I had already bonded with some of my classmates. At that school I felt like I fit in, and at this new school I felt shy and out of place.

As I entered the second grade, the kids in my new class were intimidating, cliquish, and not at all welcoming. None of these unapproachable kids had any desire to get to know me. I spent many recesses sitting alone on a bench in my brown-and-white uniform, wishing someone would play with me — just like Kathy in my 1930s life, when she spent all those lonely hours on the steps outside her home.

As silly as this might sound, there were times when I thought maybe it was my name: Julie. Nobody else I knew had that name, and I absolutely hated it. Why couldn't my parents have named me Kathy or Mary, two popular names at the time? Then, possibly, I would have fit in and the other kids would have wanted to be my friend. At the time I was just looking for any conceivable reason to justify my loneliness.

Third grade wasn't much better. By now I had turned into a withdrawn, unhappy little girl and it was hard for me to focus on learning. I was more concerned with slouching down in my seat in an effort to hide behind the kid in front of me than I was in anything the teacher had to say. I was afraid that if she called on me, I wouldn't be able to answer her question and the other kids would tease and humiliate me. My sympathetic teacher, Sister Mary Ellen, noticed that I was having a difficult time and that my grades were suffering. She contacted my parents, and together they discussed keeping me back a grade to see if that would help. Feeling that I might be a little too immature for that class, Sister told my parents that maybe I would fit in better with younger children. My parents agreed, and the following year I repeated the third grade. Later on, as I grew older, I realized that this decision was the first of two turning points that would greatly alter the course of my life.

Entering the third grade for the second time, my once-challenging situation had significantly improved. Also, over the summer I had seen the top-rated movie *Mary Poppins*, starring Julie Andrews, and knowing that I had the same first name as a big- time movie star gave me a newfound confidence.

This third-grade class welcomed me with open arms and over time, Elizabeth, the most popular girl in the class, asked me to be her best friend. This friendship helped me come out of my shell and grow my personality, and I eventually was able to feel comfortable with myself.

I have never forgotten Sister Mary Ellen's thoughtfulness and the fact that she had the foresight to keep me back a grade. Her acute interest in my miserable situation changed my life for the better, and I often wonder how different my life would have been had I not repeated the third grade.

Even though my self-esteem had improved along with my grades, the Catholic ideology taught at this school always felt odd to me. I never quite understood it completely. What I was taught always left me with more questions than any concrete answers. The priests and nuns wanted me to believe that God was always watching over me, waiting for me to commit some kind of sin so He could punish me by banishing me to the fiery pits of Hell.

Coming from a loving home, I was pretty sure that if I disrespected my parents, they weren't going to throw me into a burning fireplace. So why would God? These religious educators were teaching me to fear God. Follow those Ten Commandments, they said, or else. It was all so negative. The fact that they wanted me to believe that God would be angry and vengeful, killing babies and whole towns of people just to prove that He existed, didn't make sense to me.

Having grown up in a household that thrived in a positive environment, I had established my own concept of what God was. I preferred to believe in a loving, nonjudgmental, and forgiving God. Not one that would send a person to Hell for the slightest of offenses unless they went to confession and recited several Hail Marys and a few Our Fathers.

In the late 1960s, I was still attending this Catholic school in my junior high years. The radical pop culture, emphasizing youth and rebellion, made for very interesting times to be living in. Because my classmates and I were required to maintain a respectfully wholesome image, we felt like social outcasts living in some kind of time-warped bubble as we longingly observed the changing times pass us by.

My neighborhood friends, all attending public school, indulged themselves in the fashion craze that was rapidly sweeping across the country. The boys, wearing frayed bell-bottoms and tie-dyed shirts, began expressing their defiant side by letting their hair grow into long, unkempt hippie styles. My girlfriends were allowed to embrace the trendy designs by wearing the latest hip fashions of flared trousers, mini-skirts, and knee-high boots.

My Catholic school girlfriends and I were downright envious as we observed them in their fashionable outfits walking to school. One of the rules we were expected to live by was that our uniform skirts could be no shorter than the middle of our knees. In an attempt to rebel, my girlfriends and I rolled our skirts sacrilegiously short, all the while deludedly thinking that the nuns would not take notice.

Displeased by our lack of respect, the Sister Superior had us summoned to her office, where we were instructed to kneel on the floor in front of her so she could check the length of our skirts, which were required to touch the carpet. We nervously watched as her expression changed to anger when we did not meet her expectations. For our punishment we were required to spend a nonverbal recess sitting in the library. It was that type of restrictive behavior that had my friends and me longing for Graduation Day and the freedom to embrace and experience this exhilarating, rollercoaster time of life.

After graduating from St. Leo's, never again did I attend a Catholic Mass and neither did any of my like-minded siblings. I have no regrets at having attended St. Leo's School; my years there were truly great and memorable. I am forever grateful for the wonderful education I received, but the religious part just didn't fit for me. My disappointed parents were not at all happy about us not wanting to follow their religious way of life, but I personally felt that I had to be true to my own beliefs and explore other views besides Catholicism. (Just like Annabelle had disagreed with her parents' views about war, I did not agree with my parents' traditional belief in the Catholic religion. In both cases, our beliefs did not please our frustrated parents.)

Leaving behind my straight-laced Catholic school days, I entered my high school years in the early 1970s. My knee-high uniform skirt was rebelliously replaced with grungy, sometimes tightly painted-on bell-bottom jeans, platform shoes, and a not-so- supportive halter top.

My friends and I had so many great times cruising in our boyfriends' muscle cars to the sounds of Santana, Tower of Power, and War. On Fridays or Saturdays we could be found attending the school's sports activities, eagerly cheering for our many friends or boyfriends playing on the team to win.

During those high school years, I also experienced both love and heartache from two different boyfriends. I have to admit I really wasn't very good at playing the game of love. Having grown up surrounded by love, I was naïve and wanted to believe in a happily-ever-after relationship such as my parents had. But it took me not once but twice to learn that teenage boys had another agenda.

After graduating from Lincoln High, my

friends and I left that spirited school, taking with us our wonderful friendships and lasting memories that some of us, after all these years, still share today.

During the summer right after my graduation I was hired for my first real job, as a waitress at a Bob's Big Boy restaurant. The starting wage was $2.25 plus tips, which I considered to be good money at the time. Within the first year I was able to save up enough money to buy my first car, a classic-looking 1971 red Volkswagen Bug. Adorned with wide tires and shiny new rims, it had been lowered to give it a trendier look. My humorous father derived great pleasure from endlessly teasing me about how he thought I looked so cool driving in my car. (My solemn Civil War father called me "princess" in that life, but my fun-loving father in this life nicknamed me "Cool Jul," a name that has stuck with me throughout the years.)

That same year I was also able to afford to move out of my parents' home and move into a two-bedroom rental house, which I shared with my brother Steve. I partied hard with my coworkers that first year, and we had great fun going to concerts at the Cow Palace to hear Elton John and Paul McCartney and Wings. Taking weekend trips to Lake Tahoe for a little gambling helped us escape from the fast-paced, hectic life of a restaurant worker. In fact, I was spending so much money on fun times that it was hard to come up with the sixty-five dollars needed to pay for my half of the rent.

Toward the end of my second year working at the restaurant, I met a boy who would eventually be the man I married. He was hired to be a cook (just like the girl who came by ship to Barbados), and because I was a waitress we constantly crossed paths. At first, Steve didn't interest me in the least; he wasn't at all my type. Over the years I'd developed a bad habit of falling for the charming Romeo types, and he was as far away from that kind of guy as you could get.

My first impression of Steve was that he appeared to be standoffish and moody; in fact, some of my coworkers commented to me that they found him quite intimidating. I certainly understood why they felt that way; he was big and burly, and carried around with him a tough-guy attitude. Watching him stomp around the restaurant with a menacing scowl, I tried incessantly to figure him out. I couldn't decide if he was mad at the world or if he was just trying to act cool. As more time passed, I became increasingly curious about him and wanted to know more about what his life was like.

For some bizarre reason I saw him as a challenge, and decided that I would go out of my way to interact with him more and perhaps get to know him a little better. Like a private detective trying to solve a mystery, I began a quest to see what was truly inside his tough-guy exterior. Using every trick in my book, I made sure everywhere he went I was right there, pouring on the charm, until eventually he grew more comfortable being around me. Slowly his demeanor began to soften and a sense of who he really was began to emerge. I liked what I saw: a sense of humor and a helpful heart. I began to pursue a friendship with this enigmatic young man.

Over time I came to learn that Steve was actually very outgoing and highly self-confident, and that he reveled in the company of many friends. The quality time we now shared afforded us the opportunity to learn more about each other and as it turned out, we had quite a lot in common. We both came from large families with parents who were still married. Both of our parents had a strong belief in religion and we did not. And we both believed in working hard to get ahead in life, all the while pursuing pleasure along the way.

Slowly over the next year, Steve and I unexpectedly inched our way down a path toward love. Our almost daily interaction felt so carefree and natural that we gradually grew closer, until one day it just happened. We both instinctively knew that we didn't want to live without each other. No romantic fireworks or Cupid's arrows; just a comfortable, fun-loving relationship that we wanted to last forever. Eventually, my brother moved out of the house we had shared and Steve moved in.

Shortly after Steve moved in, someone broke into our house and although nothing was taken, this intrusive act made me anxious about coming home alone. Steve's sister Sandy, learning of my plight, knew someone whose dog had just given birth to a litter. Sandy, thinking it would be a great idea for us to have a dog for protection, surprised us with one of those newborn pups. As Sandy handed me the puppy, Steve shocked me by promptly and proudly announcing our adorable brown-and-white, mixed-breed puppy would be given the totally awesome name of Kilo (after a kilogram of weed). I reminded him that our puppy was a girl and that Kilo sounded masculine, so he begrudgingly compromised and settled on the name Kila, which he said would be short for "Tequila."

As she grew, that once-delightful little puppy turned out to be quite a mischievous handful. Kila was a unique dog and required much patience. By others' standards she was just plain crazy, but they were being generous. "Demon dog" probably was a more fitting term. Wildly stubborn, Kila was like a category five tornado, destroying everything in her path. We often teased Sandy that we would probably never forgive her for her "well-intentioned" gift. Nevertheless, Steve and I were determined to stick with this unpredictable pup and never give up. Kila was our baby; she was our crazy and we loved her.

We continued with our wild, partying ways like most kids do at that age, but over time we grew restless and bored, not only with our frivolous friends constantly loitering at our house, but with our mindless, tedious jobs as well. We felt the need for some kind of change in our stagnant, mundane lives, and we had both grown incredibly frustrated with not knowing what we wanted to do next or what steps would be needed for us to move on.

In 1976, someone must have been watching over us, because out of nowhere, one of Steve's cousins offered him a full-time job as a mechanic working on farm equipment down in Salinas. We both agreed that this would be just the opportunity we needed to slow down our life and start to grow up. With a positive attitude about what new experiences lay ahead, we packed up our belongings and Steve, Kila, and I happily headed south.

Our first six months in Salinas, known as the

salad bowl of the world, were challenging and a financial hardship for us. So much for the exciting new life we were hoping for. My precious VW broke down and died shortly after we arrived, so we were down to only one car. Even though Steve was offered more money at his new job, our rent was higher, and we hadn't realized that it might take me a while to find a job, especially without transportation.

With only Steve's income, we were so poor that for at least four days a week we ate only one meal a day, at a small, walk-up burger joint on the edge of town. At the house we were renting we had no refrigerator, so we had to make do with a small Styrofoam ice chest.

After several long, difficult months, things were finally starting to look up for the two of us. Steve got a raise, someone sold us their cheap old relic of a car, and I found a job working at the Burger Pit. Even though life in Salinas started out rough, Steve and I were both stubbornly determined to make our relationship and our new life work.

Tough times sometimes bring couples closer together, and this was most certainly the case for us. It was a time in our relationship when we were surprisingly happy, and we had come to know each other well. Together we held strong to overcome our challenges and never once did we regret the choices we had made.

Whenever possible, Steve and I spent our valued time off exploring for miles around the sprawling Salinas Valley and beyond to the magnificent mountains that embraced it. With the top off our Jeep and the sensation of the wind urging us onward, we four-wheeled through the many acres of woodlands surrounding Big Sur and went in search of the recreational opportunities at Lake San Antonio. These moments were some of our favorite times together. We couldn't wait for our sisters or friends to visit for the weekend so we could share with them the venturesome places we had discovered.

Because we were away from home a lot, we decided our dog Kila needed some form of entertainment other than the holes she was digging in the backyard, so we adopted a purebred German shepherd puppy and named our little love bug Brandy. The problem was that, after a couple of days, we found red puncture marks on our unfortunate puppy's nose. It didn't take us long to figure out that Crazy Kila had mistakenly thought Brandy was a new chew toy we had purchased for her amusement. Our weekend excursions would have to be put on hold until our poor, defenseless Brandy was older and able to fend for herself.

By 1978, Steve and I had been living happily together for almost four years. Even though we already felt married, we decided it was time to make it official, throw a big party, and make our parents happy. Steve was a no-frills kind of guy who never liked drawing attention to himself, so on August 18th, with a few family members and close friends in attendance, Steve and I went to the courthouse in San Jose and married. (In my life on the isle of Barbados I was married and in that life, just like this one, I married the cook.)

The two of us left the next morning and we headed south to our honeymoon destination of Los Angeles. We spent the week having a good time, visiting the usual tourist sites like Disneyland and Universal Studios. The following Saturday, to celebrate our wedding, we invited our closest friends and family to my in-laws' house for a backyard barbeque reception. My loving father, the talented baker, outdid himself by creating an amazingly impressive two-tier masterpiece that truly made our special day memorable. It was perfect.

A few months later, after discussing our

desires to pursue better opportunities, we moved from Salinas back to San Jose, where we both acquired jobs working with our fathers. Steve was hired as a mechanic at Di Salvo Trucking Company, where his father drove a long-haul truck. I was hired to work in the bakery department of a P.W. supermarket, where my father was the head baker. Within the following year Steve's good friend Dennis offered him a great-paying job driving tanker trucks for Chevron, and I was promoted to bakery department manager.

Finally, after six long years of worrisome financial struggles, we were both earning reasonably good incomes. By 1982 we were living the good life. Now able to buy our first home, we purchased a modest, three-bedroom, two-bath house, and we traded in our past-its-prime Jeep for a blue 1981 Corvette. We were extremely grateful for our good fortune, and proud of ourselves for all we had accomplished and for how far we had come since our days of eating at the burger joint.

As a couple, Steve and I really complemented each other well. I kept him grounded and level-headed. What I loved most about him was his strong desire to enjoy life to the fullest. No one could ever have called him boring. He was the kind of big-hearted guy who was always there for you when you needed him.

In 1985 we were able to purchase a larger house with a built-in swimming pool, and our home became the place to be for holiday barbeques and special occasions. We were two perfectly happy people.

But in August 1988, everything in our idyllic little life began to go horribly wrong. It all began when we had to put our two beloved dogs to sleep. First was Brandy, age eleven, because of an extremely painful condition that the vet called bloat. Then three months later, Kila suffered a massive stroke at age thirteen.

We were both devastated. Anyone who has

ever owned pets knows they are like your children, and to lose both of them so close together was heartbreaking. Steve took their deaths the hardest and it sent him into a depression that had me extremely worried about him. Right about that same time, two of his best friends announced that they were getting divorced. On top of all that, he felt that he was failing to make progress at his workplace and the job he once loved no longer made him happy. All of these events happening around the same time added to his sadness and to my mounting concern.

Hoping to bring some happiness back into his life, I bought Steve a new German shepherd puppy, a smart, lovable little girl that we named Nikki. At first, her lively presence seemed to help a little, but by now Steve was drinking excessively to ease his sorrow and I was at a total loss as to how to help him.

Then I started having almost-obsessive

thoughts about how I would make it financially if I were to be left on my own. I found myself mentally preparing for what I would do and how I would survive if Steve suddenly died. I tried to banish these appalling thoughts from my mind, but somehow they kept popping back up. Every time I had thoughts about him dying, I would feel awful about myself. How could I think such things? I struggled to understand why those dreadful feelings were haunting me, and I was frustrated that I could never share with anyone what I was sensing.

Lying in bed one night, I was taken aback when out of the blue Steve asked me if I thought he would die young. I told him that because of his wild and daring ways, I would probably outlive him. I left it at that, but I couldn't stop wondering how odd it was that he would ask me that question. Did he secretly know what I had been thinking? Was he experiencing his own dreadful feelings?

After some time had passed, my growing dread had me fearful to travel anywhere in our car if he was the one driving. When I expressed my fear, Steve declared that I was behaving ridiculously and that he had become extremely annoyed with me. I couldn't explain my recurring gut feelings. I most certainly couldn't tell Steve about the negative thoughts that had recently been invading my mind, or he would have wondered if there was something seriously wrong with me.

It was a chilly Sunday morning, in February of 1989, when my sister-in-law Sandy, her boyfriend Tim, her small son Joey, and I decided to take a trip to Fresno to visit my niece Christy, who had recently given birth to a baby boy. Babies were not really Steve's thing, so he had decided to stay behind and spend the day riding dirt bikes with some of his high school buddies.

After a delightful visit and a quick bite to

eat, we were on our way home when Sandy's engine began making a loud clanging noise, and then her car came to a standstill. I called Steve to tell him of our unfortunate incident and I explained to him that because of the lateness of the day we had decided to leave her car and take a Greyhound bus home. He nervously objected to our plan; he had a really bad feeling about all of us taking the bus. He strongly insisted that it would be a better idea if he drove down to Fresno to pick us up. I calmly explained that his plan was not practical, as it was already 5:00 p.m. and he had to get up early for work the next morning. I ended our conversation with "I love you," and the reassurance that I would see him later.

Moments before we were to board the bus, I heard my name being paged over the loudspeaker. It was Steve, with a last anxious attempt to convince me to not get on the bus. Again I reassured him that there was nothing to worry about. We'd be all right and I'd wake him when I got home. With that he begrudgingly hung up the phone.

It was late that Sunday night when we pulled into the quiet and nearly empty Greyhound station. Sandy and I found it eerily odd that no one from her family was there to greet us as we had arranged. We called several family members, including Steve, but no one answered their phone. My first reaction was anger towards Steve for not being home at that late hour, but when it became apparent that no one, including his parents, was at home either, we both began to feel something was terribly wrong. Worriedly we paced the lobby floor, feeling helpless, growing more anxious with each passing moment.

Finally, after what seemed like an eternity, my brother-in-law Ken arrived to pick us up. Frantically we rushed to greet him as he entered the bus station. We wanted to know why we had been left helplessly waiting, but the pale, grim expression etched upon his face stopped us dead in our tracks. We knew then that something awful had happened. As he looked me straight in my eyes, I was in no way prepared for what I was about to hear next. I stood in stunned disbelief as the words slowly and painfully rolled from Ken's lips. He told us that earlier in the evening, Steve, along with our little dog Nikki, had been involved in a horrible car accident. I was in shock and had trouble grasping the reality of what was happening to me in that moment.

We immediately left the bus station and drove the short distance to the hospital in somber silence. Nothing needed to be said, and I knew in my gut that whatever was about to happen next was going to be unbearable. It wasn't until we arrived at the hospital and I was led not to the Emergency Room, but to a door with a sign that read *Family Counseling* did I realize, "Oh my God, he's dead. Please God no this can't be happening." In that moment, time slowed to a sickening crawl.

Opening that door only revealed loud cries of anguish from the mourning family members within.

Steve died instantly in the crash that night and I was left emotionally crippled. To this day I can still remember the feelings of despair and the shocked numbness of disbelief that controlled my body from the inside out. Unless you've lived it, it's hard to explain the emotional pain you experience when in an instant you lose someone you love, someone who had been your best friend for many years, someone you had expected to grow old with.

Not wanting to be alone, I spent the rest of that night at my comforting parents' home. Unable to even think about sleep, I was consumed with the need to tell all who knew and loved Steve about this tragic loss. "How will I tell them? What can I possibly say?" He had so many longtime friends, his coworkers were his buddies, and he was such a big part of both our families. I knew with one phone call, no matter how I said it, my words were about to hurt them just as the news of his death had hurt me. Waiting until the first signs of dawn, I picked up the phone and started on my mission of gloom. Shock, disbelief, and sobs of sadness were all I could recall.

Upon arriving home later the next day, one of the first things I noticed was the phone book, lying on the kitchen table, opened to the page for the Greyhound bus station. A sudden, painful realization came over me: Steve had been on his way to pick me up when the accident occurred. He had brought Nikki along to surprise me and together they were going to the bus station to welcome me home. But as fate would have it, I was left hopeless and broken-hearted on that tragic winter's day. A few weeks later, I found out in a police report that our precious dog Nikki had survived the accident only to be run over by a car as she ran panicked through the streets. This news was just another painful blow to my already fragile existence.

With both of them gone, I was left alone to figure out how to piece my fragmented life back together again. Alone to figure out why, once again, I had known something was going to occur before it actually did. What had happened to me was crushing; it was almost like experiencing the death of my own life as I had known it. I had been a wife, and I had been a mother to my dogs. Now who was I? That fateful tragedy forever changed me and my outlook on life. Steve's death, I later came to realize, was the second major turning point in my life.

In the weeks following Steve's death, it was hard for me to come home to a house that was now empty of love. My home, once so full of life, was now quiet and lonely. No comforting sounds of Steve working on some project in the garage, no happy, wiggling dog to welcome me home. My house had always been a sanctuary, but now I lived a paranoid existence and the thought of going home alone frightened me.

I was living in a nightmare that there was no awakening from. For weeks I fearfully slept on the couch in the family room with the lights burning bright all night long. The thought of heading down the long hallway that led to the bedroom we had once shared was more than I could bear. If it hadn't been for the love and support of my sympathetic family and the dedication of some truly great friends, I don't know how I would have made it through this time of intense grief and unhappiness. (Unlike Beth's choice to live a reclusive life after the tragic loss of her beloved horse Danny, I had decided to be strong and to overcome the adversity that had invaded my life.)

Around my thirty-fifth birthday in late March, those same wonderful family and friends, concerned for my loneliness, chipped in enough money to surprise me with the most thoughtful gift anyone could have given me: an adorable, ten-month-old golden retriever puppy. The name "Shadow" quickly came to me, because from that day forward it would be just me and my shadow. That precious little girl was just what I needed to slowly start living again. I often told people that it was Steve looking down from Heaven who helped guide Shadow to me. (In my life as Beth Morgan, her dog Ruff was a constant loyal companion to her in the lonely years after her painful loss, and in the years that followed my husband's tragic death, Shadow also brought me great joy and comfort when I needed it most.)

At times when I was deeply depressed or just preoccupied by my thoughts, I would feel bad that I wasn't able to give Shadow all the attention she deserved. Shadow was an exceptional dog that seemed to sense my troubles, and in her own special way she let me know that she would be just fine.

My little daredevil taught herself to swim, and she was skilled at diving to retrieve toys from the bottom of the pool. Shadow also had her own fun way of playing ball by scooping up a tennis ball with her mouth, cleverly tossing it into the air, and then either catching it or enthusiastically chasing after it as it bounced away. This enchanting creature was quite the astute performer, and she willingly spent hours entertaining me.

Besides all the fun and games she had to offer, there was another side to Shadow that I loved most, a kind and sympathetic side. Curling up next to her on the bed during those dark days when I was especially sad, my tears dampened her fur as I kissed her angelic face. As I hugged her close, she would patiently listen as I sobbingly expressed my thoughts and feelings about everything that I had been though. Her tolerant sweetness was just what was needed to heal my grieving heart. Shadow was an angel sent from Heaven and I deeply loved that precious little girl.

A few months later, in May of that year, the savings and loan I had worked at was sold to another banking establishment. As the operations supervisor, I was expected to learn, in a brief amount of time, all of their new policies and procedures. This proved to be quite challenging as I was still in a zombie-like state from the loss of Steve and all three of our dogs. Daily I struggled to overcome the difficulties of retaining anything that I was required to read and gain knowledge of.

Then, in mid-June, I got a call at work from my neighbor Cindy, who lived across the street from me, informing me that my house was on fire. As I quickly hurried home, I kept repeating over and over again: "Oh my God, I can't believe this is happening to me." Arriving home, I was shocked to find a large part of my roof gone, a swimming pool full of burnt shingles, and a broken-down front door caused by the firemen trying to get inside. During all the commotion, my quick-thinking, thoughtful neighbors were able to rescue a confused and startled Shadow from her hiding place in the backyard. My poor little girl was a little shaken by all the excitement, but thankfully she was safe.

The fire captain concluded that the fire was caused by a neighbor who lived behind me. The neighbor had been burning leaves in his backyard on a windy day, and some of the hot ashes had blown over the fence and landed on my roof. The fire captain told me that they had smoldered for days before erupting into flames.

That fire was the final straw. I was an emotional mess. There was no way I was going to learn my new job now, so I sadly quit. I told God that I knew for some reason he was testing me, but that I was one tough girl. I was determined to prove to Him that I was strong-willed and that whatever He dished out, I could handle.

Over the next three months a construction crew worked tirelessly to rebuild my house. The stress from everything that had happened to me over the past ten months began to take an enormous toll on my health. I lost teeth, my hair started falling out, and I developed high blood pressure that I needed medication to control. (I also developed a case of arthritis, just as Beth had.)

In October, after five months off, I finally felt rested enough to go back to work. I got offered a job at another savings and loan, but the day before I was to start working there we had the largest earthquake in the area since the 1906 San Francisco quake. The tremor, located on the Loma Prieta fault in the Santa Cruz Mountains, registered at 7.1 on the Richter scale.

I was sitting at my kitchen table with a couple of my neighbors, preparing to watch the World Series between San Francisco and Oakland playing at Candlestick Park, when the disruptive event hit. My neighbor, sitting to the right of me, was the first to nonchalantly say that he thought we were having an earthquake. Having lived in California my whole life and experienced many earthquakes, I wasn't concerned, for this earthquake started out like any other. There was the slow, rolling motion, followed by the pause, and then it really started to shake unlike anything we had felt before. This was when it became abundantly clear that this was no ordinary earthquake and we needed to run.

We rose quickly to dash outside, but by now the ground shook so violently that we were incapable of standing upright. Struggling to stay on our feet, the three of us staggered as if we were intoxicated, bumping into each other and into the walls as we valiantly made our way towards the safety of the outdoors. Even though I knew what I was experiencing, the sheer magnitude of the quake overwhelmed me and made me extremely anxious in that moment.

In my Cro-Magnon life I had also

experienced this fright and dreadfulness when the earth shook. The only difference was that in this life I understood what was happening, but my poor, naïve, prehistoric family hadn't had an inkling as to what was transpiring.

As we safely stumbled out the front door, what awaited us was a sight that was beyond belief. The leafy trees that lined the street swayed back and forth as if they too were struggling to stay upright. The once-motionless cars parked along the curb and in driveways bounced from side to side as if they had hydraulics, like in those low-rider cars people drive to show off in. My befuddled neighbors were already out on their front lawns by this time, looking as dazed and confused as we were.

Just then, remembering that Shadow was still in the house, I hurriedly ran back in without any regard for my safety. I found her in the middle of the living room with her legs spread-eagled on the carpet, balancing to stay upright and unable to move. By the expression on her poor little face I could tell that she was petrified, yet I was able to convince her to follow me and we made it outside just as the shaking subsided.

The whole neighborhood remained on edge throughout the evening as we experienced several large, nerve-racking aftershocks. Everyone on our cul-de-sac stayed until late into the night, and we all shared our stories of what we had been doing at the time the earthquake hit, and how afraid we were to go back inside our homes. I chose to sleep on the couch in the family room that night, with Shadow by my side. I left the sliding glass door open wide just in case we had to make a quick break for it.

Because of my house fire, the contractors had just recently finished the repairs to my home. Now the quake had broken some water pipes in the garage, tossed to the floor several pictures that had been hanging on the walls, and shattered some plates that had tumbled from the cupboard.

By now I thought I must have some kind of curse on me. How much could one girl go through in such a short period of time? My husband was killed in a car accident, three dogs died, my house caught on fire, I had to quit my job, and now we'd had the largest earthquake since 1906. Even my friends admitted to me in a joking way that they were afraid to hang out with me for fear of what might happen next. I wondered what could possibly be left to happen. Surely I must have paid my dues by now.

Five months passed after the quake, and I was starting to half-heartedly consider that maybe the worst was behind me. My fragile core was in need of some serious healing, and my traumatized mind was in need of a peaceful existence. But how could I even contemplate moving on? I was at a loss as to where or even how to deal with the unexpected misfortunes I had lived through. The guidance and serenity that I was hoping would find me was not yet to be, for God still had one more test up His sleeve.

One morning, on my way to work, I pulled up to the stop sign around the corner from my house and waited patiently for a break in the swift-moving traffic. As soon as that opportunity arrived, I proceeded out onto the busy boulevard, when out of the corner of my eye I noticed a preteen boy on his bike swerving to avoid being hit by my car. After immediately slamming on the brakes, I was momentarily stunned when I spotted a second boy rolling off the hood of my car. A third boy, whose bike was lodged under my car tire, was off to the side looking startled.

Quickly I jumped out of my car to investigate whether they were harmed in any way. Relieved to find out that the boys were uninjured, I instantly broke down into uncontrollable sobs. I heard one of the boys, in an attempt to console me, say, "It's all right lady, don't cry." After regaining my composure, I gave the boys my name and phone number, told them to have their parents call me, and watched as they rode away on their wobbly, bent bikes. Badly shaken, I drove back home and immediately called my work to tell them what had just happened and that I wouldn't be coming in.

Later that morning, I received a call from a police officer inquiring as to what my side of the story was. I calmly explained to him that I approached the corner and didn't see anyone in either direction. When there was a break in the traffic I continued onto the boulevard. I never saw the boys until I hit them. The deep-voiced officer responded, "That sounds about right. Let me tell you their side of the story."

He said the three boys told him that they were cautiously riding their bikes on the sidewalk, got off to cross the street in the crosswalk like any law-abiding citizen would do, and then waited for a safe time to cross. They told the officer that I graciously motioned for them to proceed in front of me, and then for some reason they couldn't understand, I just careened into them. The shrewd officer stated that he liked my straightforward version better.

It was later determined that the boys were at fault. The boys were riding on the wrong side of the street and the parked cars along the curb had prevented me from seeing them. I contacted my insurance company and told them of the incident, and I never again heard any more about it.

Over time my life began to return to a form of normality that allowed peace and tranquility to heal my heart, mind, and soul. What I had learned through meditation was that people who had lived through some kind of adversity, and who had chosen to accept their life and all that had been given them not by wallowing in sorrow, but by learning and growing from their life lessons, they were indeed the fortunate ones. Every obstacle in life was an opportunity to grow on a soul level and for some, suffering could bring you closer to God. Now, when I look back at those difficulties that I would not have wished on my worst enemy, I would not change a thing. Those moments were important for my spiritual awakening and probably more important than all of my happiest moments.

Reflections

According to the New World Encyclopedia, reincarnation (from Latin meaning "to be made flesh again") in religion and philosophy refers to the belief that a part of a living being, the soul, survives death to be reborn in a new body. This reincarnated self carries with it some essence or identity of the past life into the next life, although the self usually is not aware of it. Reincarnation is a central tenet of Hinduism, Buddhism, and many theosophical and New Age groups.

The concept of reincarnation goes back some 3,000 years to India and Greece. A poll conducted for the Sunday Morning television program ("Reincarnation: Believing in Second Chances," Sunday Morning, CBS News, KPIX, San Francisco, May 15, 2011) shows about one in five Americans believes in reincarnation, and roughly one in ten remembers a past life.

After much reflection on my past life regression sessions and my unusual encounter with the unknown, I decided to write this story because of my own life's unusual twists and challenging turns, and because what I'd learned from my riveting hypnotic sessions led me to believe that our souls persevere.

I began by delving into some noteworthy details about the characters in my stories to see if I could uncover historical facts relating to a few of my past lives. I was determined to find any trace of solid evidence that would prove not only to my psyche, but to all those doubting Thomases as well, that what I had experienced was real. My research left me both frustratingly disappointed and mind-blowingly surprised by the results.

My Internet research on the lives of Annabelle Conner, from Civil War-era Georgia, and Elizabeth Morgan, champion horseback rider, found no conclusive evidence that they had ever existed. Having little patience when it comes to computers, I grew increasingly disillusioned with every unproductive roadblock I encountered. Perhaps if the professor had asked me for more detailed information, I could have been able to recall Annabelle's father's first name. If I had been made more aware of the region in which Beth Morgan competed, this information would have aided in my search. Extremely dissatisfied by this unfortunate turn of events, I decided to persevere, and made one more attempt by looking up the history of Barbados. To my surprise, in one short click of the mouse there it was, right before my eyes: the proof I had been so determined to find.

I read with much eagerness the pertinent information I had just found on the first settlers of Barbados. The reference piece (http://www.accessbarbados.com/barbados_histor y.php) stated that in 1625 Captain John Powell landed and claimed the island for England. Two years later, his brother Captain Henry Powell landed with a party of eighty settlers and ten slaves, and with enough equipment to start a new colony. More settlers followed in their wake and by 1628 the population had grown to around two thousand.

What an amazing find! Ships sailing from England to find new land: check. There was a captain named John Powell: check. Waiting two years for the ship to return with enough supplies to start a colony: check. "More than ecstatic" was the only way to describe how I felt about the discovery of this information that was so relevant to my story. Even though I was not one hundred percent successful in all of my research, this was just the breakthrough I needed to remain open-minded.

While writing this book and reflecting on the uniqueness of each individual life, I began to take notice of a gradual developmental process, which made me consider that the concept of evolution of the soul was in fact true. It become clear to me that from each of my lives, a small fraction of either my personality or of a life-altering experience appeared to have been carried over and blended into my current life, to make me who I am today.

For example, in my life today, I never gave birth to any children. I was never opposed to the idea, my husband Steve did not seem to care one way or the other, and I never really felt the maternal instinct to have a child that so many other women experience. While reflecting on my past lives, I realized that each time I was a female, I never had children. Was my lack of a maternal instinct something that I had somehow carried over from my past lives? This parallel between my current life

293

and the past lives I'd had as a woman made me curious.

Then I noticed something else. Not only did I die from hunger as Annabelle, but I also starved to death in the Middle Ages dungeon when the king caught me and my friends stealing his precious possessions. In my prehistoric life, although I died in a volcanic eruption, my family and I were always anxious and concerned about hunting our next meal; the need and desire for food was a huge part of our precarious existence.

When I recalled my Civil War life, I commented to the professor that there was an interesting parallel between Annabelle having been subjected to starvation in her final years and my love of food in my current life. I have always had a constant desire to eat and it has been an ongoing struggle throughout this life to keep my weight down. Growing up, I ate constantly and quickly, almost as if I was subconsciously making up for all the food that I had been deprived of in my other lives.

And then there was my life as Kathy in 1930s New York — I wanted so badly to play kickball out in the street with the other children in the neighborhood, yet because of my uncompromising mother I was never allowed to. When I mischievously disobeyed her and ran out into the busy street anyway, sadly I was struck by a car and killed. In my current life, one of my favorite things to do when I was a child was to play ball in the street with my brothers, sisters, and the other neighborhood kids. There, on our quiet, traffic-free little street, my accommodating parents allowed me to play freely.

While reviewing the tapes of my hypnosis sessions and assessing each person's set of characteristics, it was Annabelle's personality I connected with most. As Annabelle, I was spoiled and overly self-confident, and I thought very highly of myself. In fact, I was downright conceited. Annabelle had a way of enchanting her generous father into getting her the pretty things she wanted. In my current life, I found that my charming sense of humor has pretty much worked to my advantage. In my family, I am thought of as the stubborn one who always wants things my way, and if I don't get it I have a tendency to pout and then forge ahead until I do.

To further provide evidence of the evolving soul, while I was researching the life of John Powell I learned that prior to his voyage, his occupation was that of a slave dealer; he probably treated his cargo unsympathetically. (I wonder now if this is why he didn't go to the garden, but instead lingered in limbo before moving on.) Captain Powell used his ship for transporting slaves from Africa to England before he was commissioned by the king to find new land. Upon his return trip to the island, his brother Captain Henry Powell made Barbados the first British settlement in the Caribbean to possess enslaved Africans.

While reflecting on this knowledge, I contemplated how the object lessons our souls acquire during a lifetime are carried over from one life to another. That was when I began to try to link the life lessons together. Because my Civil War life and my Barbados life had both involved slaves, I noted that over the ages my soul, which had at one time belonged to an unsympathetic slave trader, during Annabelle's life had evolved her spirit into a more compassionate individual who had respect for slaves and considered them to be a part of her family.

Years later, with my soul now evolving once again, I haven't a prejudiced bone in my body. I am someone who has throughout my life believed in equality and compassion for all people. This conjecture led me to the conclusion that the soul's evolution could be a combination of past life experiences, personalities, and the gradual advancement through knowledge that the soul absorbs along the way.

What I experienced under hypnosis was very believable to me. Throughout the entire event I felt as if I was bringing up distant memories that had been stored somewhere deep in the recesses of my mind. For the longest time it was very difficult for me to imagine how I could have come up with such detailed information if I had not experienced it for myself. The colors, the sounds, and the feelings were all there, yet my conscious mind still questioned the reality of these memories.

It wasn't until I found that the life in which I ventured across the seas to find new land closely matched the history of the Barbados settlement that I become a true believer. I know what I saw and I know what I felt, and no nonbeliever will be able to take that away from me. People can talk you out of your assumptions and viewpoints, but they can't talk you out of your experiences. That is why I have the utmost assurance that somewhere deep inside me, a well-traveled soul exists.

I wrote this story not to persuade people into believing in reincarnation, but to simply make people think. Death is a taboo subject and many people ignore the existence of death in a hope that it will never happen to them. Nevertheless, if more people took the time to research and educate themselves on what it will mean to them personally when they die, it would make death easier to accept and they would be less afraid when the time finally comes for them or their loved ones.

And when that time does come, do we just cease to exist or does our soul live on? Do we go to heaven, where God awaits us with loving arms? Do we merely vanish from existence, as if our lives never had meaning? Or is death merely a transition and an adventure to a new life? Open your heart and your mind to the many possibilities. There is so much to learn and there are so many beliefs to choose from. What I have come to believe from my experience is that if you live a good life, love unconditionally, and respect others and treat them with kindness, there's a strong possibility that you will at some time be reunited with loved ones, including your beloved animals.

After one's passing, a peaceful heavenly atmosphere will surround you, and in some cases you will be immersed in inexplicable beauty for as long as it takes for you move on to your next life. I am no longer afraid to die because I trust that with my passing I will enter into a profound peace and a renewal of life.

From this whole enlightening experience I became more aware of the astuteness of my inner voice, which never stops talking. And I have learned to trust that this guiding force is a tutor of valuable lessons I must learn. When I'm filled with doubt about the course my life is on, I simply remind myself that whatever unfolds, it's part of God's greater plan He has for my life, and that I am always where I'm supposed to be, doing what I'm supposed to be doing.

Through hypnosis, I was given the glorious gift of being in what I perceived to be the presence of God and of knowing that our lives are so much more than one dimension. One of the most powerful messages I received came from the Light itself and all its infinite wisdom. I was told that every experience in my journey is an opportunity for spiritual growth if I choose to see it that way. Even though I may not understand the "why" of an unsolicited event, I should look for its gifts at the end of a long struggle. I must "trust" that I am cherished. I must "trust" that I am stronger then I assume myself to be, and that I can and will overcome anything. And if I listen quietly to the voice within me, I can still hear the magnificent Light reassure me: "Trusting and believing in my words will lead to a future that never needs to be worried about."

Our beloved Julie
left this world
peacefully, yet too
soon. Her spirit will
live on in all of us.

"Embrace every
chapter of your life"
- Julie Brand
3/22/54 - 8/10/14

Made in the USA
Las Vegas, NV
13 March 2021

19508070R00174